CU00839214

Introduction to

Criminology

Russell Pond is a magistrate in Lincoln having also served as a JP in Birkenhead. He is a member of the Executive Committee of the Lincolnshire and South Humberside Branch of the Magistrates' Association and a member of the Lincolnshire Police Authority. He obtained a law degree from London University while working in what was then Rhodesia and was later awarded an MSc in Criminal Justice by the University of Leicester. *Introduction to Criminology* stems from his belief that many people—including criminal justice practitioners and students who have not (or have not yet) studied criminology—would benefit from a straightforward introduction.

Introduction to Criminology
Russell Pond

ISBN 978-1-872870-42-7 (Paperback)
ISBN 978-1-908162-26-7 (Adobe PDF ebook)

Published 1999 by
Waterside Press
Sherfield Gables
Sherfield on Loddon
Hook, Hampshire
United Kingdom RG27 0JG

Telephone +44(0)1256 882250
E-mail enquiries@watersidepress.co.uk
Online catalogue WatersidePress.co.uk

Reprinted 2012

Main UK distributor Gardners Books, 1 Whittle Drive, Eastbourne, East Sussex, BN23 6QH. Tel: +44 (0)1323 521777; sales@gardners.com; www.gardners.com

Cataloguing-In-Publication Data A catalogue record for this book can be obtained from the British Library.

e-book *Introduction to Criminology* is available as an ebook and also to subscribers of Myilibrary and Dawsonera.

Printed by Lightning Source.

Introduction to

Criminology

Russell Pond

WATERSIDE PRESS

Introduction to **Criminology**

CONTENTS

CHAPTER

Acknowledgements

I am indebted to my wife for great patience when I should have been doing things around the house, to the staff of the Scarman Centre for the Study of Public Order at the University of Leicester for their excellent teaching and to Bryan Gibson who, rather to my surprise, thought the book a good idea and has guided me throughout.

Russell Pond
May 1999

CHAPTER 1

Introduction

The issue of free will versus determinism is *the* key to resolving any argument about the causes and cures of crime . . .

James Bidinotto (1989)

It is probably true that most people have a resistance to "ologies'; often perceived as academics answering questions that no one has asked. This is certainly true in relation to criminology. 'Criminologists don't live in the real world; they need to spend a day in court, policing the streets or supervising offenders . . . and to see what it's really like', is not, I hope, an unfair paraphrase of a view not uncommon among criminal justice practitioners.

Of course, we are all aware of, and concerned about, the crime rate. We all know, or think we know, what should be done about it: more severe sentences (and, yes, of course 'prison works'); more policeman on the beat and a return to that respect for authority such as there once was—all this will contribute to less crime. These are self-evident truths— or are they? Perhaps they come closer to hunches which we have never thought about too carefully. As David Garland (1997) writes:

> Intuitive, "instinctive", common-sense views about crime and criminals are still more persuasive to many—including many in positions of power and authority—than are the results of carefully executed empirical research.

To read and consider some of the theories about the causes of criminal behaviour and to examine critically some of our cherished beliefs about criminal justice requires a certain amount of intellectual courage because we will be in areas that are not only strange but, perhaps, a little frightening—and we may meet with ideas that will challenge some of our basic notions about society itself. To take a few examples at random:

- society itself creates criminals by its reaction to certain behaviour (labelling theory)
- criminality is natural: it is non-criminal behaviour that has to be explained (control theory)
- the law is created by the powerful and favours the powerful so making criminals of the powerless (conflict theory); and
- criminality is the result of some biological imbalance (biological positivism).

Just as someone may be a perfectly adequate car driver without any idea what happens under the bonnet—but is a better motorist if he or she has a passing knowledge of mechanics—so will people who are involved in the criminal justice arena be better equipped if they have some idea of theoretical criminology and matters related to it. It is upon that belief that this book is based.

WHAT IS CRIMINOLOGY?

The very word 'criminology' was not coined until 1879 when it was first used by the French anthropologist, Topinard—the first British textbook on criminology is barely 40 years old. Before that date, important work had been done: we still owe a debt to such writers as Beccaria (1738-1794), the statisticians Guerry (1802-1866) and Quetelet (1796-1874), and Lombroso (1835-1909) and Ferri (1856-1928) of the Italian School, to all of whose work we would now attach the name criminology.

A simple but adequate definition of criminology—although not without its critics—is 'the scientific study of crime'. It is this notion of criminology being a *science* that causes difficulty for some commentators. There has always been a fundamental question whether the *natural sciences*, for example, biology, chemistry and physics, should accept the *social sciences*, like criminology, as being scientific in the same sense. In the school days of many of us, the natural sciences were seen as precise, certain, quantifiable and measurable, while the social sciences—because they are essentially about people—could never attain these heights, largely due to the fact that they had so many competing explanations for phenomena. However, not only do many of the natural sciences and their laws now seem more random than we could ever have imagined, but writers like Thomas Kuhn (1922-1993) have attacked the old notions about scientific truth and progress and shown that competing explanations are just as much a part of the natural sciences as the social sciences. Paul Feyeraband (1924-1984) showed that there was a difference between what scientists *do* and what they *say they do* and called science 'sloppy' with no particular method. If we think of science as meaning a method of investigation rather than a body of fixed knowledge, then assuredly criminology *is* a science. Gibbons (1994) actually writes:

> Much of what passes for theorising in criminology involves fuzzy or undefined concepts, propositions that are implicit rather than explicit and/or that are internally inconsistent, and kindred other problems of exposition or logical structure.

The next thing to note is the multi-disciplinary nature of the topic. Contributions have been made to criminology by psychologists, psychiatrists, statisticians, economists, nutritionists and architects, to name just a few. As Paul Rock has observed, some of the contributors have been 'passing through on their way to other goals'. Thus criminology is, in some respects, a 'mish-mash' and this needs to be understood—but this adds to its fascination as a topic of study.

This leads us directly into what subject areas should actually be covered in an introductory handbook of this kind. Arguably, theoretical criminology is only of value if it informs what we might term, as a catch-all, 'criminal justice'. This term covers all those subjects that appear in the main textbooks including the work of the criminal courts and the judiciary, crime and punishment (including such items as its justification and efficacy), white collar crime, public disorder, victimology, statistics about crime, the role of the police and crime prevention.

Criminology should not be thought of as a subject that has proceeded in a linear progression from some early fumblings through stages of increasing knowledge into a sunlit upland of understanding. Its competing paradigms, from whatever century, continue. The great Italian scholar Cesare Beccaria (1738-1794) of the Classical School—in his book *On Crimes and Punishments* published in 1764—wrote 'There must be a proper proportion between crimes and punishments'. He seems to have been the first writer to articulate the premise that the punishment should fit the crime which, some 200 years later, became a central feature of the Criminal Justice Act 1991 with its 'just deserts' approach to 'commensurate' (often dubbed 'proportionate') sentences. When Ron Clarke (a one-time doyen of writers connected with the Home Office Crime Prevention Unit) introduced situational crime prevention he founded it on the idea that crime is the result of rational choices based on the perceived risk of being caught compared with the perceived rewards of getting away with it. In this, he was also echoing the classical theorists. But a word of warning is necessary. David Garland (1994) points out that we must guard against the 'recovery of tradition' and not be too keen to discover in any new element 'added to the criminological armoury' that it really originated in some eighteenth or nineteenth century idea. He writes:

> criminology is a socially constructed and historically specific organization of knowledge—grounded in a particular set of institutions and forms of life.

Some broad signposts
Before embarking on an investigation of some of the theories that are the bedrock of criminology, it might be useful to have certain signposts in mind:

- 1750-1870 *Classicism*: based on human beings having a rational mind and free will, sometimes called 'voluntarism'
- 1870-1960 *Positivism*: human behaviour is based on forces over which we have little or no control, sometimes called 'determinism'
- 1960s *Interactionism*: criminality resides in the response to certain behaviours; and
- 1970s *Radicalism or critical criminology*: the ruling elite stigmatises certain behaviour as criminal.

Mention should also be made at the outset of perceived differences between the sexes and crime, something which is dealt with more fully in *Chapter 6*. According to Eileen Leonard in *Women, Crime and Society* (1982) it is:

> . . . odd that half the population should apparently be immune to the criminogenic factors which have lead to the downfall of so significant a proportion of the other half. Equally odd it is, too, that although the criminological experience of different countries varies considerably, nevertheless the same differentiation remains.

We should also note, cautiously, what Paul Rock wrote in *The Present State of British Criminology* (1988), i.e. that 'the criminological mind has sensed the exhaustion of theory and turned to the practical and empirical'. One of the reasons that

> theoretical criminology is dying a death amongst the younger generation . . . is because of the way research is funded and theory itself has been transformed by the brutal facts of riots and urban disorders, by the general victimisation revealed in crime surveys and in particular victimisation of women . . . crime now looks more sober, abundant and distressing . . .

Finally, in his *Principled Policing* (1998) John Alderson writes:

> The mysteries of philosophy sometimes resemble a moveable feast, during which philosophers appear to be in permanent dispute.

It would not be too much of an exaggeration to substitute 'criminology' for 'philosophy' and 'criminologists' for 'philosophers'.

THEORIES OF CRIMINOLOGY

We can now start to look at theories of criminology and the way in which these can contrast and conflict with each other—starting with the great divide between 'classicism' and 'positivism'. The next chapter looks at classicism (including, for example, social contract theories and utilitarianism), then at the work of Cesare Beccaria before assessing where classicism stands today. *Chapter 3* outlines positivism in its various forms and *Chapters 4* and *5* look at control theories and strain theories respectively—both of which are generally thought of as falling under the same school of thought.

The book then moves on to deal with a range of other key theories which are central to a basic understanding of criminology. These I have identified within the following broad bands: gender, subcultures, labelling and differential association (all of which are dealt with in *Chapter 6*); conflict and radical criminology (*Chapter 7*); and victimology, fear of crime and restorative justice (*Chapter 8:* where I also draw attention to the significance and use of statistics).

I hope that this analysis will enable the busy practitioner or newcomer to criminology to get to grips quickly with the basics, free, at this stage, from the debate, contention and wealth of detailed materials which necessarily underpin more advanced studies. It is perhaps something of an understatement to say that at almost every juncture there is room for argument of one kind or another. My simple aim is to allow the reader to become familiar with the topic and its terminology and to realise why dismissive remarks of the kind noted at the start of this chapter are short-sighted. To this same end, I have tried, in *Chapter 9, Criminology: Aspects of Criminal Justice* to demonstrate how theory impacts on everyday practice.

At the end of each chapter (or in the case of *Chapter 9* at the end of each topic) I have added what I hope are useful *Key Points*. This is again with the idea that with a topic so wide-ranging and often controversial as criminology it will prove profitable if newcomers can keep the bare bones in mind when looking back over a chapter, comparing other theories outlined in the book, or considering fresh scenarios or new developments. I hope that this approach will serve to whet the appetite—and thus encourage the reader to explore some of those more expert works listed in the *Bibliography* at the end of the book.

CHAPTER 2

Classicism

> Crime is understood as a product of free will; a course of action freely chosen through calculation of the pain and pleasure involved. Its control is assumed to lie in better and more efficient means of punishment. Establishing specific causes of crime or trying to understand its meaning is of little or no concern.
>
> (Muncie *et al*: 1996)

The classical school of criminology (I shall call it that although some writers insist that it is not 'criminology' but rather a 'criminal justice philosophy') emerged from the period—around 300 years ago—known as the Enlightenment. This is described by Wayne Morrison (1995) in felicitous phrases as:

> A great coming out party, where after a great deal of behind the scenes preparation, and confusion on the night man came of age and was free to go out into the real world a free man to make his own destiny.

Behind classicism lay social contract theories and utilitarianism.

The social contract
This is an unwritten agreement between the state and its citizens—who are equal in every way—in which the rights and duties of each are expressed. The 'golden age' of social contract theories was between about 1650 and 1800, but they have made a come back now and again and, in the last 30 years, prime ministers of both of the major political parties have appealed to the concept.

Before the Enlightenment, monarchical regimes had assumed a right to govern but this was now challenged and in the words of John Locke it was 'voluntary agreement that gave political power to governors'. Thomas Hobbes (1588-1679) wrote in *Leviathan* (1651) that 'the right of all sovereigns is derived from the consent of every one of those who are to be governed'. Hobbes believed that in a state of nature man would be involved in a 'war of all against all' and life would be 'nasty brutish and short'. To avoid this, people should freely subject themselves to an absolute ruler or institution, a Leviathan.

In contrast to Hobbes' somewhat pessimistic outlook Rousseau (1712-1778) took the view that in a state of nature men were equal and free and it was the complex forms that society took as it developed that corrupted them. Rousseau is particularly remembered for his idea of the general will, that the citizen body is sovereign and for the opening words of his book on the social contract: 'Man is born free and everywhere he is in chains'.

John Locke (1632-1702) could, not unjustly, be called the father of materialism. He believed that natural law gave man rights to life, liberty and property (which appealed to the emerging merchant class) and it was the government's task to protect these rights. He thought that no one should accumulate more land and goods than they needed and this would ensure a rough sort of equality, but that the invention of money had meant that some people could now accumulate more of the earth's resources than they needed.

It might well be asked 'What are these long dead philosophers to do with criminal justice?' The answer is that underlying the whole law and order debate are two different and largely competing views of the nature of human beings. What we might call the 'conservative' perspective— authoritarian, with an emphasis on punishment and a philosophy that the more severe that punishment is, the greater will be its deterrent effect, and with emphasis on police powers and the rule of law—is very much Hobbesian in outlook. By contrast, the 'liberal' view is more open or tender minded, with emphasis on rehabilitation and the removal of the social causes of crime and a desire for social justice—and follows in the footsteps of Rousseau.

The social contract's relevance to criminal justice can be summarised as follows:

- humans had originally existed in a state of nature, grace or innocence; to emerge from this state required the application of *reason*, and that meant that both the meaning and consequence of actions were understood
- the will, which regulates and controls behaviour, is a psychological reality and is generally *free* though it *may* be influenced by God and the Devil and, more down to earth, by a desire for food, sex and security
- there is a right to inflict punishment—transferred, though it is, to the state
- the principal instrument for controlling behaviour is fear, particularly fear of pain; and
- punishment is the chief way of creating fear so as to control behaviour.

This also reflects more modern views that a person who chooses crime— as a 'moral actor' with free will–and who exercises an unfettered choice when he burgles a house or steals from a shop should be punished or deterred accordingly. This view contrasts with the positivists' view of the actor (see *Chapter 3*)—who is someone who has lost control and who is beset by forces within or external to himself or herself and which he or she can do little about.

These are "two equally abstract images of humanity, each a caricature of reality" (Young 1994).

Utilitarianism

We now need to look at the work of Jeremy Bentham (1748 to 1832) whose pleasure/pain principle and whose epigrammatic 'the greatest happiness for the greatest number' are well known. His importance to present discussion lies in his principle that the punishment that the law imposes should result in pain in excess of the pleasure that might be derived from the criminal act, so as to be a deterrent. But if the pain was too much in excess then that would reduce 'the greatest happiness' and be contrary to Bentham's principle.

Bentham was a great advocate of prison as a punishment—'a mill for grinding rogues honest', as he called it. At the time that he was writing, prison tended to be used mainly for those awaiting trial and transportation. Bentham suggested a panopticon, the characteristics of which were:

- a circular building with a glass roof and cells on every storey
- every cell visible from a central point
- the manager of the prison would employ prisoners in contract labour; and
- cells backlit so that the prisoners were watched without them knowing at any particular moment whether or not they were being watched; or, to use Foucault's (1991) chilling phrase, 'one is totally seen, without ever seeing'.

The structural idea of such a prison is long forgotten but the philosophy that accompanied the panopticon, discipline and surveillance is not. Who could read Foucault's description and not be reminded of the CCTV cameras that have become part of our lives, so much so that the expression 'Panopticon Mall' has been coined to describe shopping centres.

CESARE BECCARIA

Beccaria, or to give him his full name, Cesare Bonesana, Marchese de Beccaria, seems to have been a not particularly brilliant student in eighteenth century Italy, but one who had an interest in mathematics, which was to serve him well in his future as a university professor. In 1763, he was asked, as an assignment, to write an essay on penology, a subject about which he apparently knew nothing. With the help of two brothers, one of whom was an official of the prison in Milan, he completed the essay in 1764, the year that it was published as *Dei Deliti e Delle Pene (On Crimes and Punishments)*. The book was published anonymously for fear of possible repercussions and it was condemned by the Catholic Church for its rationalistic ideas. Nevertheless, it was soon translated into 22 languages and, when the first English version appeared, three years later, the translator wrote of it 'perhaps no book, on any subject, was ever received with more avidity, more generally read, or more universally applauded'.

What was in this extraordinary book by a 26-year-old? We have to remember that it was written at a time when severe and barbaric punishments were commonplace, torture was rife and capricious judges added punishments at their personal whim, as well as taking the part of their own class in its struggle against others. The French Revolution, which was to provide a climacteric for such struggles, lay only two decades into the future.

Beccaria's book was essentially about the reform of the criminal justice system in order to make it more logical and rational. Many of its ideas resonate with our own understanding of the ideal criminal justice system of today:

- men have sacrificed a portion of their liberty so as to enjoy the rest in peace and security. The sum of those portions sacrificed make up the sovereignty of the nation
- but this is not enough, because these portions must be defended against individuals who try, not only to withdraw their own share but that of others. Some tangible motives must be introduced to prevent this and these motives are the punishments established against people who break the law
- a punishment that exceeds the limit fixed by the law is just punishment plus further punishment—so a judge or magistrate cannot augment the established punishment
- the true measure of crime is the harm done to society not what was intended by the person who committed it
- there must be a proper proportion between crimes and punishments
- punishment will attain its end when the evil that it inflicts only exceeds the advantage derivable from the crime
- the more promptly punishment follows on the crime the more just and useful it will be
- one of the greatest curbs on crime is not the cruelty of punishments but their certainty; and

- to prevent crimes the laws must be clear and simple and the entire nation united in their defence.

Even bearing in mind the earlier warning by Garland, (see *Chapter 1*) about the 'recovery of tradition' it is well worth noting that Beccaria was something of a radical for he wrote:

> What are these laws that I am supposed to respect ... Who made these laws? Rich and powerful men who never deigned to visit the squalid huts of the poor, who have never had to share a crust of mouldy bread ...

Beccaria's thinking much influenced the French Penal Code of 1791. Penalties were fixed absolutely and no latitude given to the judge as a result of any difference between individuals. First offenders, recidivists, children, adults and the insane were all treated the same. The later Penal Codes began to move away from this 'pure' form of classicism as it became clear that individuals were not all alike and not equally responsible for their actions. A range of experts were now advising the court of what degree of reason could be expected from an individual and what mitigating circumstances there were. We see this today in our own courts: by and large, up to the end of the prosecutor's (or Crown) case, classical principles are being applied—but in the defence case, particularly when it comes to sentencing and pre-sentence reports are involved, we see the influence of positivism (for example the defendant's offence is partly explained by the fact that both his parents died when he was young and he has been out of work for many years).

Neo-classicism

These ideas grew to produce what is known as the neo-classical school which not only embraced the idea that there were differences in the degree of reason between individuals but also that imprisonment was an environment that could actually exacerbate criminal tendencies; the same sentence could have different effects on different people:

> The neo-classicists took the solitary rational man of classicist criminology and gave him a past and a future. They merely sketched in the structure which might blur or marginally effect the exercise of voluntarism. It is this model—with minor corrections—which remains the major model of human behaviour held by the agencies of social control in all advanced industrial societies ... It was against this model too, that the positive school of criminology attempted to exert its influence.

(Taylor, Walton and Young: 1973)

Classicism today

Where stands classicism today? As already indicated, we can roughly date the growth of positivism, and hence the decline of classicism, at least temporarily, firstly to evolutionary theory that contended that human behaviour is actually no different to animal behaviour, expressed by, the aptly named, Tiger and Fox (1971) as 'propensities for behaviour are in the wiring' and the writings of, among others, the English psychiatrist Maudsley and the prison doctor, Thomson, but above all those of Cesare Lombroso (1836-1909) who was indebted to them, and later to his disciples of the Italian School.

However, as I have suggested, classicism is still influential in some of the theories to be examined later in this book.

- the 'drift' theory of David Matza, which asserts that when young offenders drift between criminal and non-criminal behaviour it is through the exercise of free-will that they choose the former
- the 'control' theory of Travis Hirschi is largely based on the notion that people do not commit crimes because it is in their best interests not to, i.e. they exercise a rational choice
- even radical criminology takes a classical stance when it 'restores the authenticity of the deviant act'—people seen as deviant or criminal are in fact behaving quite rationally given their particular circumstances and the social context (mindless violence is rarely, if ever, 'mindless')
- on the other side of the political divide, writers like the American James Q Wilson, echo the classical approach. Wilson writes:

  if legitimate opportunities for work are unavailable, some people may turn to crime, but if criminal opportunities are profitable, some persons will not take the legitimate jobs that exist.

We have seen that classicism may be enduring but it has serious problems:

- it is based on the assumption that all men are free, rational, and equal but we know that the real world is very different and, as the social contract is about defending rights and liberties to acquire wealth and property for example, massive inequalities are built into the system
- if men act rationally, as we are asked to believe they do, then why is there still so much crime: why does reason not prevail?
- if all are equally endowed with reason why do the poor regularly commit more crime than the rich?

- classicism's emphasis on free will suggests that biological, psychological and social circumstances play little or no part in criminal behaviour
- the whole notion of rationality is impenetrable: we know full well that we all act irrationally at times and, in any case, is rationality fixed for all times and all circumstances?
- essentially classicism is an 'armchair' theory: it can produce no empirical data in its support.

A final thought before we look at positivism:

> The period of classical criminology is often down played in criminological books . . . This is wrong. We have never moved on from the dilemmas which classicism contains.
>
> (Wayne Morrison)

•   •   •

Chapter 2: Classicism—Key Points

- Crime is seen as a product of free will: an action freely chosen.
- Underlying classicism are social contract theories and utilitarianism.
- The social contact is an unwritten agreement between the citizen and the state.
- After the Enlightenment in the seventeenth century the right of monarchical regimes to govern was questioned.
- To Locke it was voluntary agreement that gave governors their power.
- Hobbes believed that in a state of nature there would be war of all against all so that people should freely subject themselves to an absolute ruler, a Leviathan.
- Rousseau in contrast thought that in a state of nature men were free and equal and that it was society that corrupted them.
- We see these two views reflected in the law and order debate: the essentially pessimistic Hobbesian view of the 'conservatives' and the more 'liberal' softer view in the footsteps of Rousseau.
- Locke contended that it was the natural law that gave men the right to life, liberty, and property and that government should protect those rights.
- Social contract theory taught that humans emerged from a state of nature by the application of reason and that the will was generally free: there was a right for the state to inflict punishment which was the chief way of controlling behaviour through fear.

- Bentham in his utilitarian theory believed in the greatest happiness for the greatest number and from this that the pain of punishment should exceed the pleasure from crime but not by much.
- Beccaria wrote about the reform of the criminal justice system and was the first to propose a proper proportion between the crime and the punishment. He influenced the French Penal Code of 1791 but initially all offenders were treated the same.
- Neo classicism recognised the differences between individuals both in terms of their ability to reason and that the same sentence could have different effects on different people
- Classicism declined in the face of evolutionary theory (see *Chapter 3*) but remains highly influential.

CHAPTER 3

Positivism

> For us, the experimental method is the key to all knowledge . . . for us the fact governs and no reasoning can occur without starting with facts. For us science requires spending a long time in examining the facts one by one, evaluating them, reducing them to a common denominator, extracting the central idea from them.
>
> Ferri (1901)

According to an oft quoted phrase, 'positivism's major attribute is its insistence on the unity of the scientific method' (Taylor, Walton and Young, 1973). This means that all those methods that have been successful in studying the physical world are equally valid in the study of man and society. Positivist criminologists have sought to discover 'scientific' laws through measurement and quantification, and have acclaimed objectivity and scientific expertise and found criminal behaviour in the law-governed nature of human action through forces of which the wrong-doer is unaware. In this endeavour they have created a mirror image of classicism:

- free will has disappeared under determinism;
- equality bows before natural differences and expert knowledge; and
- human laws that are created become scientific laws that are discovered.

The major single influence in the growth of positivism is usually seen as Charles Darwin (1809-1882). From the time of his evolutionary theory classical thinking became 'prescientific'. Human beings were animals and were subject to the laws of nature just like all animals. All true enquiry was scientific.

The examination of positivism will be divided into biological, psychological and social positivism. But they must not be seen as inhabiting separate worlds: indeed Lombroso, the father of biological positivism came to embrace social ideas.

BIOLOGICAL POSITIVISM

Because this is a substantial topic it will help the reader to have an outline of the subjects which will be covered. I will begin with what might be called the early biological theories, although some of the direct successors to Lombroso will be mentioned, then I will follow Sheldon's theory of body types. After that will come the examination of genetic factors both uninherited and the more important group of inherited factors where I will examine families, twin studies and adoptees. This is followed by a brief discussion of the vexed matter of intelligence and crime, and the section finishes with a somewhat longer one on biochemical factors and their relationship.

Early biological theories
Historically speaking, the first attempts to bring to bear the armoury of science on the problems of crime were social rather than biological. It has been suggested that the change from classicism to positivism was spearheaded by the 'moral statisticians'. The work of Quetelet and Guerry, which will be referred to later, stemmed from social statistics and for half a century after them positivism remained in a sociological vein. It was with Lombroso, in 1875, that the focus moved from the social to the individual. This marked the movement of the medical men into the field of crime and the corresponding ousting of the sociologically minded. After this the history of criminology was rewritten as a branch of medicine.

In the 1760s Johan Caspar Lavater (1741-1802) published a large work on physiognomy in which he linked facial features and behaviour. We no longer believe in linking particular conduct with weak chins, shifty eyes and so on . . . or do we? A development of Lavater's work came from Frank Joseph Gall (1758-1802) and his follower Spurzheim who publicised his work in Britain and America. This was the 'science' of phrenology. Gall and Spurzheim believed that the exterior of the skull conformed to the shape of the brain, that the mind consisted of faculties which were related to the shape of the brain and, therefore, the skull, so that 'bumps' were indicators of the faculties. Specific parts of the brain controlled behavioural activities. For example, destructiveness was to be found just above the ear and overdevelopment could lead to violence and murder. Such propensities could be held in check by the intellectual faculties—and so a person's conduct was due to whichever of these pulls was the strongest. It was even suggested that a child could be trained to strengthen the desirable faculties.

It is worth noting that it was Gall who first distinguished the grey and white matter in the brain, and in 1995 Bullmore *et al* reported that the sharpness or otherwise of the boundary between them was linked to certain mental conditions.

The work of Lavater and Gall illustrated the popularity of biological explanations for crimes and there may be two reasons for this. Firstly, it meant that the causes of crime lay not *in society* but rather *in individuals*, so no responsibility fell on governments, and secondly non-criminals could take a certain comfort from the fact that they were not in any way like criminals, who were clearly different.

This point was developed, at least in his early writings, by Cesare Lombroso (1835-1909), who, with Ferri and Garafalo, was to make up the famed Italian School of Criminology. Lombroso, who graduated from the same University as Beccaria, but 100 years later published his great work *L'Uomo Delinquente* (*The Criminal Man*) in 1876 (by the fifth edition it had grown in size eightfold!).

Lombroso is largely remembered for the idea that there is a physical criminal type. His theory is one of degeneracy (a point previously made in Britain in the 1860s by Maudsley and Thomson): the physical characteristics of criminals were an indication of this degeneracy. Criminals were throwbacks to some earlier evolutionary stage and to such people Lombroso attached the term 'atavistic'. He listed a number of what he called anomalies which indicated the atavistic person. Among these were: a large jaw; ears of unusual size; a twisted or upturned nose; a receding chin and arms of excessive length. After examination of a number of Italian criminals, Lombroso came to the conclusion that five or more anomalies indicated a 'born criminal'. He also compared anomalies of the skull in criminals with non-criminals using, probably—for the first time in criminological research—a control group. In later editions of his book Lombroso was to include many other items that he saw as related to crime causation. Some of these, like sex and marriage practices, banking practices and church organization might seem strange to us, but he had moved away from purely biological factors.

With the support of the Home Office and with the aim of refuting Lombroso's claims of a physical criminal type, Charles Goring undertook research in which he examined over 3,000 criminals and a similar number of non-criminals. His book *The English Convict: A Statistical Study* was published by HMSO in 1913. Goring was unable to find any significance in the sort of anomalies on which Lombroso had relied, so he was able to write 'There is no such thing as a criminal type'. But he did find that criminals were one or two inches shorter, three to seven pounds lighter and of lower intelligence than non-criminals. He also suggested that crime would continue as long as criminals were allowed to propagate, a view not welcomed in official circles. He did, however, make a significant contribution with his idea that criminality is a variant of normality differentiated by degree only. His belief that criminality is 'normal' rather than 'pathological' was to prove important. He believed that there is a criminal characteristic common to all individuals: he termed this 'the criminal diathesis' (a condition of the body making it liable to specific diseases).

As a word of warning, the work of E A Hooton and his *The American Criminal* should be mentioned here. His study was well financed and he undertook Lombrosian type measurements with great attention to detail. One of his findings was: 'Low foreheads, high pinched nasal roots . . . compressed faces and narrow jaws, fit well into the picture of general constitutional inferiority'. Criminals, he found, were inferior to civilians in nearly all bodily measurements. He was also able to conclude that '. . . tall thin men tend to be murderers and robbers; tall heavy men are killers and also commit forgery and fraud; undersized men are thieves and burglars'. In fact Hooton's work is an example of thoroughly bad science. He believed in biological inferiority and he set out to demonstrate it, for not particularly creditable reasons and, of course, he did. He did not specify what 'inferiority' was or what standards he used. In 1941 another writer using biological standards was actually able to show that Hooton's criminals were a considerably more advanced group biologically than his non-criminals. Hooton also advocated the segregation of the criminal population into a self-contained area with closed in-breeding. He ended that extraordinary passage with the words: 'It would be quite essential to keep out extraneous politicians, criminologists and uplifters'.

Turning to the other members of the Italian triumverate: Enrico Ferri (1856-1928) proposed that crime was caused by a number of factors:

- physical (race, climate, temperature, seasonal effects);
- individual (age, sex, psychological condition); and
- social (density of population, customs, economic conditions).

As a socialist he subscribed to the view that crime could be controlled by improving social conditions and that the state was the instrument through which this could best be done. He advocated inexpensive dwellings for workmen, better street lighting, birth control and provision for public recreation among a long list.

Because of his political activities he was dismissed from the University of Pisa, founded the Socialist paper *Avanti* but resigned from the party in 1924 and wrote favourably about aspects of Mussolini's Fascist government.

The third of the great Italian positivists is Garofola (1852-1934). He attempted a definition of crime which would have universal application and '. . . would designate those acts no civilised society can refuse to recognise as criminal and repress by means of punishment'. He called these 'natural crimes' which would violate the two basic altruistic sentiments of probity (respect for the property rights of others) and pity (revulsion against the infliction of suffering on others). In a chapter of his *Criminology* (1880) entitled 'The Law of Adaption' he outlined a theory of punishment which would eliminate those whose behaviour showed that they were not adapted to civilised society. These included death, and partial elimination, by which he meant life imprisonment or transportation. He considered that this satisfied the deep seated public demand for the punishment of criminals simply because they had committed a crime. Not a far cry from a view well rehearsed today.

Body types

Very much in the Lombrosian tradition are those writers who have tried to show a link between different types of build and personality. In the 1940s William Sheldon examined the nude photographs of some 200 young men and was able to classify them into three basic body types. Morrison (1995) tells us that few other scholars were able to understand by what insights Sheldon achieved this! The somatotypes, as Sheldon called them, together with the accompanying personality types were:

- *endomorphs:* large and heavy, sociable and outgoing;
- *mesomorphs*: broad and muscular, adventurous and aggressive; and
- *ectomorphs*: thin and bony, restrained and introverted.

Because nobody can be entirely characterised as any one of these somatotypes, Sheldon devised a scale running from one (lowest) to seven (highest). A totally balanced person would be 4-4-4 and a person with strong mesomorphic tendencies might be 3-6-2. Sheldon concluded that most delinquents tend towards mesomorphy and that criminal groups have slightly more endomorphs but lack ectomorphs. His typical delinquent was 3.5-5.6-2.7. These claims were later tested by the Gluecks (1950) whose research upheld Sheldon's claims. They found, for example that in their institutionalised delinquent group 60 per cent were mesomorphs. In 1972 a further attempt by Cortes and Gatti using more sophisticated methods of measurement rather than looking at photographs found over 50 per cent of delinquents were mesomorphs.

In the Summer 1997 edition of the *British Journal of Criminology*, two Swiss criminologists reported on a study of nearly 1,000 juveniles between the ages of 14 and 21 years. While the self-report questions were being completed, interviewers were asked to rate respondents as athletic, frail/weak/feeble, fat/soft or hard to classify and also apparent aggressiveness (determined by the interviewers deciding whether they would be afraid of having a serious argument with the person). They concluded that the athletic constitution was linked to more aggression towards other children at elementary school age and that the same was true for an appearance of aggressiveness. The physical attributes offer (or remove) opportunities: violence might indeed be feasible for those who wish to impose their will on others. It seems that in the case of most boys sometime between the ages of 10 and 15 years they learn to react more constructively in difficult encounters.

In the absence of anything like a feasible biological explanation, what are we to make of the work of people like William Sheldon? Certain points can be made:

- the broad, muscular, aggressive person is the perceived stereotype of a criminal; it may be that this is the type that is more likely to be selected as a possible offender at each stage of the criminal process;
- all the delinquents in Sheldon's study were institutionalised; these are not necessarily typical of the criminal population as a whole but are simply the ones who have been caught; and
- we know that the poor and deprived are over-represented in institutions. Perhaps those are the very factors that produce a certain type of body build.

Genetic abnormalities
A normal male has an X chromosome from his mother and a Y chromosome from his father. There are 23 pairs of chromosomes that carry the inherited factors and one of these pairs is the sex chromosome: in the normal female, XX and in the male, XY. In a very small percentage of people there is an extra chromosome which can lead to abnormal sexual characteristics. Abnormal males can be XXY, known as Klinefelter's syndrome and probably unrelated to criminality, or XYY. It is this latter classification with its 'extra maleness' which conjures up a picture of the 'super male', more aggressive, more criminal. It has certainly been suggested in a number of studies that the extra Y is associated with violent and criminal behaviour and has been pleaded as a mitigating factor in a number of criminal trials. Chromosome abnormalities have caused considerable discussion. One of the difficulties that proponents of the idea have to face is that thousands of perfectly normal people exist who have an extra X chromosome. The link with criminality is unproven though there may perhaps be a link with some psychiatric disorders.

Inherited genetic factors
One question to which an answer must be sought is whether dysfunctional traits like criminality or feeble mindedness can be inherited in the same way as eye colour or blood-type. There are no convincing answers.

Family studies
A number of studies have purported to show that both criminality and feeble-mindedness run in families. In *The Jukes*, published in 1877, Richard Dugdale came across six offenders related by blood. He traced a further 1,200 and found a high incidence of crime, pauperism, prostitution and illegitimate births. In 1925 Henry Goddard wrote *The Kallikak family*. He traced over 500 descendants of the liaison between an American soldier and a feeble minded tavern girl. He showed to *his* satisfaction a high incidence of feeble-mindedness, illegitimacy, alcoholism and some, but not much, criminality. He was satisfied, though he changed his mind later, that feeble-mindedness was inherited and so too was criminality. It seems that the decision to classify people as 'feeble-minded' was taken on sight and was 'hasty and dubious'. In addition, Stephen Jay Gould (1996) has recently shown that a number of the photographs in Goddard's book purporting to show feeble-minded members of the Kallikaks, have been retouched to make them look 'diabolical'. Nothing in either work does anything to demonstrate a link between crime and inherited factors. Environmental factors may be far more important, with ideas about criminality being learned.

This leads to the important question whether heredity or environment causes crime—and how to disentangle such factors. Two methods have been attempted: twin studies and studies of adoptees.

Twin studies
To answer the question posed above, it is clear that a way needs to be found to hold one of the two variables, heredity or environment, constant. If similarities in criminality are then discovered it would seem that this is related to the constant, whereas differences would be connected with the variable. This is possible through research on twins and, ideally, those separated at birth because, if with a separate environment criminal behaviour was shown to be the same, the case for inherited criminal tendencies would be proved. There is of course a snag; twins are rare enough, never mind those separated at birth. There are two types of twins known as: MZ (monozygotic), or identical twins, from a single egg; and DZ (dizygotic), or fraternal twins from two eggs, who, genetically, are like any other siblings. The theory ran that if one MZ twin was criminal and criminality genetically transmitted the other twin would also be criminal, i.e. a concordance of 100 per cent. There would be no such relationship between DZ twins whose behaviour would be discordant. If, however, criminality was related to environmental factors, results would be similar for both MZ and DZ twins.

The early studies, such as that by Lange (1929), showed a concordance for MZ twins of 77 per cent and for DZ twins of 12 per cent.

Ideally, of course, the MZ twins should not have shown a discordance of 23 per cent nor the DZ twins the 12 per cent concordance. Environment could not be ignored. Another interesting finding was that where there was concordance some had committed entirely different types of offence leading to the conclusion that though a predisposition to crime might be inherited, the form that the crime took may be dependant on other factors. All the early studies laboured under methodological difficulties: in most cases at least one of the twins was institutionalised, so was unrepresentative and the tests to determine whether the twins were MZ or DZ were crude.

In 1968 Christiansen used the official twin register of Denmark in his research. He separated out serious crimes and found a greater concordance for these than for lesser crimes (1974).

All these results are thought provoking, even if the majority view is that they are far from conclusive. The challenge of separating heredity and environment seems insurmountable: it has been pointed out that identical twins are treated more alike than fraternal twins, so any similarity may be more to do with shared experience than genetics.

Adoptees
Studies of adoptees depend on finding children adopted at birth and then discovering if there is a correlation between the criminality of the adoptive and the biological father and the adoptee. If the biological father has a criminal record and the adoptive father has not then, if there is a genetic influence, one might expect the adoptee to show a propensity to criminal behaviour.

Rennie (1987) showed that if the biological father is non-criminal then it appears to make little difference if the adoptive father is criminal or not. If the biological father is criminal then about twice as many adoptees are convicted of a crime before adulthood. But there are still difficulties to be faced with these results. One is that adoption agencies try to place children in homes with a similar environment. Mednick *et al* (1987) refer to a correlation between the adoptive parents' socio-economic status and the biological parent. Even allowing for this, they conclude that 'biological parent convictions are significantly related to adoptee convictions'. On the other hand, Trasler (1987) writes: '. . . this area is a methodological minefield because of the complex and unexplicit policies of adoption and fostering agencies'.

Intelligence and crime
Is there a link between low intelligence and crime? Without going into the controversy surrounding IQ tests and what they do or do not measure, what is not in doubt is that a number of reputable studies have

shown a disparity between convicted offenders and 'normal' people of about eight points. This may be due to a number of factors, for example:

- the less intelligent may be more likely to be caught; and
- those with lower intelligence may find it harder to resist agreeing with the police and thus are easier to convict.

David Farrington (1994) finds that the underlying link between intelligence and crime may be due to the ability to manipulate abstract concepts. Those who are poor at that tend to do badly in intelligence tests. Hand in hand with that goes a poor ability to see the consequences of offending and the effects on the victim. Such people may then be less likely to be deterred from crime. It may be also that those who do poorly in such tests at school tend to be ignored, do badly at school as a reaction to being 'labelled' (see *Chapter 6*), and then are more prone to criminal behaviour on leaving school.

Biochemical factors
A wide variety of what I will term 'biochemical factors' have been associated with criminal behaviour in some way or other.

Sexual hormones
In the popular mind, testosterone has long been associated with males and hence with aggression and even violent behaviour. As long ago as 1947, Beaman divided into two a strain of fighting mice he had bred and castrated those in one group. They ceased to be fighters until they were given an injection of testosterone after which they fought as much as the control group. Later research on monkeys suggests a relationship between environment and hormonal balance since Rose *et al* (1974) showed that a change of social setting affected testosterone levels. One of the problems is that early research failed to distinguish physical and verbal aggression. Schalling (1987) has shown that high testosterone levels in young males are associated with verbal not physical aggression. Olwens (1987) has suggested that high levels of testosterone cause low levels of tolerance resulting in readily provoked aggressive responses.

In women, low levels of circulating progesterone may lead to pre-menstrual tension and mood swings. Although there is no evidence that this or menstrual symptoms actually cause crime they may possibly accentuate personality traits.

Adrenaline
Adrenaline levels are linked with cortical arousal which is itself linked with fear and excitement. Mednick has suggested that violent criminals take a stronger stimulus to arouse them but, once cortical arousal is

achieved, they recover more slowly and this results in a loss of ability in learning to refrain from undesirable behaviour. Baldwin (1990) partly links the reduction of crime with age to arousal rates. Criminal behaviour becomes less and less stimulating in that there is less cortical arousal and consequently less pleasure is derived from it.

Blood sugar
Low blood sugar levels may lead to irritability, mental confusion and violence. Shoenthaler (1982) has described experiments where lowering the intake of sugary foods in the diet of institutionalised persons has reduced the levels of violence. The regular imbibing of alcohol in large doses can lead to low blood sugar levels and aggressive behaviour.

Cholesterol
Some evidence has been adduced that criminals have very low cholesterol levels and such levels have been related to difficulty in internalising norms.

Allergies
It is possible that allergic reactions to drugs and foods (particularly certain additives) may lead to behavioural changes. The so-called 'Twinkie defence' reduced murder to manslaughter on the grounds of diminished responsibility in a case in 1987 in America, where the defendant pleaded a chemical imbalance in the brain caused by eating junk food, in his case a surfeit of Twinkies.

Vitamins and minerals
Deficiency in Vit B Co has been associated with hyper-activity in children and some criminal behaviour, B1 with aggression and B3 with acts of immorality because of an impaired ability to distinguish right from wrong. The toxic effects of lead are now widely accepted and these may include behavioural changes. Research in Illinois has shown that high levels of copper and low levels of zinc are much more likely to be found in violent than non-violent people. Walsh (1997) used a combination of additives to improve the absorption of zinc from certain foods and reports improvement in behaviour after two months. He is convinced that a genetic predisposition to a chemical imbalance plays an important part in determining whether a child becomes anti-social. (*The Times*, 20 July 1997)

PSYCHOLOGICAL POSITIVISM

... Certain types of personality may be more prone to react with anti-social or criminal behaviour to environmental factors of one kind or another. This is not to accept the notion of "crime as destiny" ...

Hans Eysenck (1987)

I will now examine those writers who have searched for the causes of crime *in the mind*. In other words, is there a criminal personality?

Personality

First, we need to try and arrive at a working definition of that elusive idea, *personality*. Marshall (1994) calls it 'what a person brings to a situation that belongs to them'. It differs from *attitude* because that is object specific: directed towards specific people or things, in contrast to personality which is a broader term. Someone's behaviour is a function of his or her personality (or attitude) and a situation. As Marshall points out, sometimes one will be dominant, sometimes the other, while at other times there will be a balance. If the situation is, let's say, a fire behaviour is likely to be the same whatever the person's personality.

The distinctive feature of a personality trait is its persistence, stability and predictability: given a certain stimulus the response can be foreseen. Hans Eysenck (1916-1992) started from the belief that our ability to be conditioned by environmental stimuli (like Pavlov's dogs who salivated when they saw a light because they had been conditioned to associate it with food) is genetically transmitted. He propounded three dimensions of personality which he called introversion—extroversion (E), neuroticism (N) and psychotism (P). These dimensions were dependent on the cortex and the autonomic nervous system. A person who is at the extrovert end of the 'E' scale is cortically under-aroused and therefore seeks stimulation, which can result in offending behaviour, while the introvert who is cortically over-aroused avoids stimulation. That person develops inhibitions about certain types of behaviour from conditioning. Someone who is highly neurotic (high N in Eysenck's terms) has an autonomic nervous system which reacts strongly to unpleasant stimuli. This interferes with the process of conditioning, in contrast to individuals with very stable autonomic systems.

Eysenck measured personality, largely through questionnaires, and found that high Es were outgoing, sociable, optimistic people while high Ns were anxious, moody, and sensitive. Psychotism is rather more difficult to characterise but it seems to include insensitivity to other people, lack of regard for danger and aggressiveness. Eysenck suggested that people with a personality that reflected a high E, high N and high P score would have anti-social inclinations. Later work has attempted to link scores with particular offence types: violent and property offenders have lower N scores than other groups and con men have lower P scores. Eysenck's work has many critics. Some have doubted the existence of the 'fixed core personality' that lies at the heart of the theory; others, for example do not accept the idea of genetic transfer of conditioning. There is a problem with E scores because they measure two factors which may be termed 'impulsiveness' and 'sociability'. Only the first has any connection with criminal behaviour; and so a high E score may be due to any combination of components. Other researchers have produced results that seem to support the method. McGurck and McDougal (1981) showed that 30 per cent of delinquents and no non-delinquents in a sample showed a high E, high N cluster, and 12 per cent and none respectively, a high E, high N, high P, score.

Sigmund Freud

I now turn to the work of Sigmund Freud (1856-1939) who divided the personality into:

- *the id:* these are the primitive biological drives which are illogical, immoral and pleasure seeking. They include: food, drink, warmth and sexual pleasure
- *the superego:* this involves those values that are internalised in interaction with other people but most importantly with parents. It is what is referred to as 'conscience'. The development of conscience is important in what the sociologists call 'socialisation', the process by which we learn to become members of society internalising its norms and values (largely, though not exclusively, in childhood and, as indicated, from parents) and learning to perform our social roles; and
- *the ego:* this part of the personality is concerned e.g. with memory, perception and thinking—and balances the demands of the *id* and the *superego*.

Freud provided us with two models of criminal behaviour. The first is mental illness. Under this head Freud includes crimes like rape and arson. The second cause of crime, according to Freud, is a weak conscience. Support for this view can be found in other research, for example *Wayward Youth* (1925). August Aichorn called those with underdeveloped superegos 'latent delinquents'. He treated them, in contrast to borstal type regimes which he thought only made the problems worse, by providing them with a happy and pleasant environment which fostered good relationships with adults to facilitate socialisation and the formation of a superego.

Upbringing

In 1936, Healy and Bronner examined 105 families with two sons—one criminal and one non-criminal—and concluded that many of the criminal sons had failed to develop emotional ties with the parents and had weak consciences. This brings me to a brief consideration of the relevance to criminology of the bringing up of children and the effects of families, a subject to which whole volumes have been devoted.

It can be noted that the 'Cambridge Study' by West and Farrington (1973) showed that less than five per cent of families were responsible for over half of all criminal convictions in the study. The sad fact is that 'problem children' tend to grow up as 'problem adults', and problem adults tend to produce more problem children (Farrington: 1994).

John Bowlby (1907-1990), whose theory of maternal deprivation has been highly influential, although nowadays much less so, considered that a 'close unbroken relationship with the mother is essential to the mental health of the child' and that separation accounted for most permanent cases of delinquency. Various criticisms have been made (sometimes about things that Bowlby never said concerning his theory, for example he never claimed that it would account for *all* offending behaviour). His methodology has been attacked on the grounds that his sample of 44 thieves referred to his child guidance clinic was not a representative one and that his control group of 44 children, similarly referred, but not for thieving, was never checked out for thieves. Other critics assert that there was no evidence that deprivation was irreversible and that the whole theory concentrates too much on the role of mothers.

In the 1980s Hall Williams was able to say 'The myth of maternal deprivation has been exploded'. Michael Rutter (1981) made the point that it is not maternal deprivation that is so important but 'privation'—where upbringing is lacking in some way.

The husband and wife team, the Gluecks (1950), showed that fathers of offenders provided discipline that was generally lax and erratic with physical punishment common and praise rare, while those of non-offenders used physical punishment less often. Their discipline, by contrast, was firm and consistent. The Gluecks preferred the idea of the 'under the roof culture' that moral and emotional conditions had more effect upon behaviour than maternal deprivation.

The term 'broken home' is emotive and such a background is often considered to be a major cause of crime, but the evidence is unsatisfactory. The Glueks, on the one hand, found in their sample that twice as many delinquents came from broken homes as others, but Ivan Nye (1958) found less delinquency in broken homes than in unhappy unbroken homes. The sociologist, Baroness Wooton, attacked the notion of the broken home when she pointed out that no agreement had been arrived at by writers as to what they meant by the term, that there was no evidence about the frequency of broken homes in the general population, and that all homes are eventually broken up for one reason or another. Perhaps the last word should be left with West (1969):

> Socially deprived, unloving, erratic, inconsistent and careless parents tend to produce badly behaved boys.

It will not have escaped notice that girls did not figure 30 years ago!

SOCIOLOGICAL POSITIVISM

> There is sufficient evidence to suggest that the high crime rate of Britain's inner cities is matched by high rates of offender residences.
>
> Susan Smith (1986)

In the third broad division of positivism we come to sociological positivism. To reiterate from *Chapters 1* and *2*, positivists rejected the classical emphasis on free will and instead looked for factors which caused human beings to act in a way over which they had little or no control. We have already looked for those factors in the body and in the mind (*Biological Positivism* and *Psychological Positivism* above) and now turn away from individual propensities to commit crime and look at society as the cause. This also takes us to the fascinating study of environmental criminology sometimes called the geography or the ecology of crime; and I will examine the spatial distribution of offences and the spatial distribution of offenders—in simple language, where offences happen and where offenders live. First, however, I must turn briefly to Emile Durkheim (1858-1917), a 'rather forbidding figure' as Frank Parkin calls him. Parkin continues '. . . it is not easy to picture Durkheim relaxing over a drink or laughing aloud at something funny'. His writings, it has to be said, reflect the man; but he is particularly important for two reasons:

- **Sociology as science**
  Durkheim was insistent that the facts of social life are no different in principle from the facts about the physical universe, so that the same methods of study should be employed. To Durkheim social facts were to be considered as natural things. Society as social phenomena were actual entities existing 'out there' and external to individuals.

* **Law and order**
  Durkheim considered crime to be an ineradicable feature of
  society: and, indeed, it was a normal part of a healthy society.
  Deviancy, he considered, had a function in pushing forward the
  frontiers of morality and in 'boundary setting': without deviants
  who would know what was normal. Crime is the price to be paid
  for the possibility of progress. In a well known passage he wrote:

  > Imagine a society of saints, a perfect cloister of exemplary individuals.
  > Crimes, properly so called, will then be unknown but faults which seem
  > venial to the layman will create there the same scandal that the ordinary
  > offence does in ordinary consciousness.

Environmental criminology
Returning to the theme of environmental criminology, this idea has a
long history, going back at least as far as Quetelet (a Belgian
mathematician) and Guerry (a French lawyer) who working separately,
but nearly at the same time, on examining the first set of national
criminal statistics in 1827 postulated 'a constancy of crime'. They were
each struck by the fact that annual totals of crime remained strangely
constant and that the contributions made to the overall figures by
various crimes hardly fluctuated at all. In addition they provided a link
between crime and geographical location because real variations
remained constant. It was as if some factors other than the propensities
of individuals were at work.

Chicago
The story then shifts to Chicago and the Sociology Department of the
University between the two world wars. Chicago was the place for
sociologists to be: a little town with a population of 10,000 in 1860 had
become a city of two million people by 1910. This staggering growth was
largely due to an influx of immigrants from all over the world, each
influx bringing a recurring series of problems, including low wages, long
hours, bad working conditions and poor housing: 'everything in a state
of agitation'.

Two important basic concepts were introduced by Robert Park, a one
time newspaper man who was destined to become head of the
University's sociology department. He viewed the city as more than a
place but a kind of social super organism in which there were many
'natural areas' where different types of people lived. His second basic
concept was that just as a new species of plant might invade an area,
come to dominate it and drive out other life forms so the same process of
'invasion, dominance and succession' could be seen in human societies.
This latter idea was explored by Ernest Burgess (1916) who pointed out

that cities do not grow just at the edges but radially from the centre in concentric rings which he described as 'zones'.

Briefly stated: *Zone 1* is the central business district; *Zone 2* is 'the area in transition', being invaded by *Zone 1* as it expands (the invasion, dominance, succession process), so that the properties are deteriorating and occupied by the poorest class, often recent immigrants; *Zone 3* is where the homes of the workers are who have established themselves and moved from *Zone 2; Zones* 4 and 5 are residential districts and the commuter belt, respectively.

Of course, no city exactly replicates this concept, not even Chicago, where the zones on the eastern side stopped on the shores of Lake Michigan, but the idea gave birth to an important theory.

The Work of Clifford Shaw and Henry McKay

Chicago suffered from an ever increasing crime problem in the 1920s, the era of prohibition. Shaw and McKay investigated this and other matters in their *magnum opus, Juvenile Delinquency and Urban Areas* which can still be read with profit more than 50 years on. They drew a number of maps:

- *spot maps:* that showed the residences of juveniles (aged 10 to 16 years) involved at some stage in the criminal justice system: they also prepared similar spot maps reflecting a variety of other social problems
- *rate maps:* in which they divided the city into square mile areas and showed the percentage of the total juvenile population in the system; and
- *zone maps:* which indicated clearly that the closer to the centre the greater the problem.

From their work they made two central claims, i.e. that:

- the crime rate in a particular area remained constant despite the vast changes in the inhabitants. Those who indulged in criminal behaviour became law abiding as they moved away from the centre; and
- crime problems went hand in hand with social problems. Where the crime rate was the highest there would be found the highest rates of infant mortality, suicide and truancy together with certain economic factors, a high percentage of families on welfare, low rental housing and a low rate of home ownership.

This led Shaw and McKay to a theory of 'social disorganization' as a cause of crime. Essentially this seems to mean a lack of standards, a lack of social control, a lack of cohesiveness in the society which leads to criminal behaviour being tolerated and accepted. Their work has been highly influential, but is not without its critics, e.g.:

- it depended upon statistics gained from official records to measure delinquency (as we shall see in *Chapter 8*, these are far from reliable indicators of *real* rates of crime)
- the second criticism concerns the 'ecological fallacy'. This states that ecological correlation is almost certainly not equal to its corresponding individual correlation. As an example, some English research in the 1960s showed that recorded crime rates were highest in areas with a relatively high rate of ethnic minority immigration (an ecological correlation) but on an individual basis those immigrants had a fairly low rate of offending (individual correlation) (Bottoms, 1994).

In the 1970s environmental criminology received a fresh impetus from what Bottoms calls 'the rediscovery of the offence'—i.e. that where delinquents reside (high offender rate areas) is not always where they commit offences (high offence rate areas)—and a growing understanding of the importance of 'the operation of the housing market'. In this latter connection Terence Morris had earlier, in 1957, shown that the zonal hypothesis was not applicable where high offender rate council estates were located at a considerable distance from the city centre. The notion of invasion, dominance, succession was modified by social policy.

High offence rate areas
In 1991 in an areal study of Stockholm, Wikstrom showed, perhaps not surprisingly, that there was a positive correlation, on an areal basis, between the burglary rate and the percentage of householders with a high annual income. This he called 'target attractiveness'. But this concept itself can be divided into two, a lucrative target and an absence of surveillance of that target.

This leads us to an all too brief mention of the 'routine activities theory' largely the work of Marcus Felson (1992):

> The probability that a violation will occur at any specific time and place might be taken as a function of the convergence of likely offenders and suitable targets in the absence of capable guardians.

In other words for a burglary to be committed there must be:

- a likely offender
- a suitable target

• an absence of capable guardians.

It is this last item which becomes increasingly important as work and social life means that people spend more and more of their time away from home, which in turn may result in an increase of crime against unattended residential property.

Another interesting contribution in this area comes from Patricia and Paul Brantingham (1981) who postulated that life patterns might influence the location of offences. They suggested that we all have 'cognitive maps' in our heads of the cities in which we live. Some areas we will know very well—where our home is, around our work place, and where we shop for example—while some areas we hardly know at all. They suggested that, leaving aside the opportunistic crime, most offenders will not commit crimes in areas that they do not know. The Brantinghams claim that offences will occur where 'criminal opportunities intersect with cognitively known areas'. In a similar vein, it is also interesting to note that Forrester *et al* (1988), in their research into burglaries in the Kirkholt estate in Rochdale, found that 63 per cent of burglars questioned said that the distance they travelled to the target house was less than a mile. The authors concluded that 'domestic burglary in Rochdale takes on an almost claustrophobically local aspect'.

The housing market
In 1967 Rex and Moore introduced the concept of 'class struggle for housing'. They examined the difficulties faced by immigrant families in the Sparkbrook area of Birmingham, finding that building societies took an unhelpful view of mortgage applications and that the council operated a five year waiting period for houses. The result was that immigrant families were forced into privately rented multi-occupation areas like Sparkbrook, and other 'twilight areas'. In 1970 Lambert took this idea further in another area of Birmingham which had a high crime rate. He showed that this was not due to the newly arrived immigrants but the 'long stay' residents, black and white. However, the crime rate among the immigrants grew until it matched the area as a whole. It thus seems that the explanation for crime does not lie in the nature of an area itself; but in the difficulties that specific groups experience because they are obliged to live in that particular area. This is much what Shaw and McKay (above) were saying.

In 1989 Bottoms *et al* examined two low rise council estates in Sheffield. They were about the same size and only separated by a road. They had been built at about the same time and there were no statistically different demographic factors (age, sex, class, earnings). But there was a 300 per cent difference in recorded crime as between the two. One of the estates, Stonewall, had begun as a 'good' crime free area and had remained so, the other, Gardenia, had started out just the same but had 'tipped' in the 1940s into a high crime rate area. The research was unable to explain the 'tipping' (a matter to which we return below), but considered that the local authority's housing allocation policy had maintained the difference between the two areas. Those in severe housing need had been allocated to Gardenia as had those who had relatives living there. The housing allocation process was tending to bring to the two estates those with a different propensity to commit crime. It is important to note that it was not suggested that there was a direct link between housing allocation and criminality but rather that it was due to the interaction of the residents and the perceptions of outsiders.

Bottoms revisited this research in 1992 and found that the homeless were being allocated to both estates and there was some convergence between the two areas.

Broken windows
It has been shown that 'tipping' from a low crime rate area to a high rate area can happen quickly; and that once the process begins it often accelerates. This brings us to the 'broken windows' hypothesis of Wilson and Kelling (the progenitor of the 'zero tolerance' policing of the 1990s).

Wilson and Kelling believed that disorder in an area, broken windows left unattended, litter accumulating, graffiti unremoved, what they called 'incivilities', disturbed the informal processes of social control. Residents would prefer not to do anything and the increasing air of neglect would make the area fair game for theft and vandalism. Wesley Skogan supported the hypothesis and suggested that disorder sparks concern about safety among the residents and this may even lead to crime: it undermines the stability of the housing market and leads to 'good' residents moving away. With this seemingly attractive idea there needs to be contrasted the arguments of Roger Matthews (1992), amongst others, which have cast doubts on the progression from incivilities to crime, something which seems unproven. Finally, Rosemary Mellor writing in 1989, illustrated the importance for the criminologists of the future of this area of study with her comment that 'localism *and* mobility defines everyday life'.

Multiple victimisation
Richard Sparks (1977) carried out the first British review of household multiple victimisations. His work showed that reported figures were highly skewed in that although many residents had not reported any crime against them some had reported a significant number. The original *British Crime Survey* (1992) showed that 71 per cent of all offences

reported had happened to respondents who had been victimised more than once during the year. These figures are without regard to any specific type of crime (for example victims of domestic violence are very likely to suffer more than once: see for example Genn, 1988 who reported on the lives of many women in severely deprived areas who suffered sexual and physical assault from men with whom they had some sort of relationship and pointed out that these were largely lost from view in most surveys). Turning specifically to burglary a Dutch study showed that one-third of domestic burglars returned to the same house to commit a further offence. Bottoms (1994) suggests possible reasons for this:

- if a property is particularly vulnerable, e.g. it is close to a main road, it is detached, then routine activity theory would suggest that different burglars might be attracted to it
- the same burglar might well come back
- discussion with others about good targets might stimulate another burglar.

In a study on Merseyside, *New Insights Into Repeat Victimisation* (Johnson, Bowen and Hirschfield, *British Journal of Criminology*: 37:224-241) the authors show that the observed rate of victimisation within one month of a previous incident was 15 times the expected rate, but by six months it had dropped off to 2.6 times the expected rate. This, they suggest, might be due to the occupier of a once burgled house installing better protection, which often takes a few weeks to arrange, but might also be explicable by the fact that a burglar might simply forget a good target, particularly if he is 'doing' several houses a week. This they illustrate by showing how poor the contextual memory of all of us usually is.

• • •

Chapter 3: Positivism—Key Points

- Positivists embrace the idea that the methods of studying the physical world are valid for the social world.
- Positivism is deterministic: people are in the control of forces of which they are unaware.
- It was influenced by the work of Darwin: human beings were subject to the laws of nature like animals.

Biological positivism

- The earliest attempts to apply science to crime were social rather than biological but with Lombroso in the late nineteenth century criminology became a branch of medicine.
- Lombroso, a member of the Italian School, believed that there is a physical criminal type and this was an indication of degeneracy: he used the term 'atavistic' and listed a number of 'anomalies' of which the born criminal had five or more. Later he was to move away from purely biological factors as a cause of crime.
- In 1913 Goring showed that there was no such thing as a criminal type and suggested that criminality was 'normal' not 'pathological' and criminal characteristics were common to all (the 'criminal diathesis').
- Ferri proposed that factors causing crime were: physical, individual and social. He advocated better dwellings for workmen, better street lighting, etc.
- Garafola referred to 'natural crimes' that all civilised societies would punish which violated the two basic altruistic sentiments of probity and pity.
- Sheldon divided young men into body types: endomorphs, mesomorphs and ectomorphs and found that delinquents tended to be mesomorphs. This finding was confirmed by the Gluecks.
- It has been suggested that genetic abnormalities may have links with criminality: some studies contend that an extra male chromosome may lead to an aggressive male criminal person.
- Another area of study has been whether criminality is inherited like, for example, eye colouring.
- The work of Dugdale and Goddard—both of whom studied family histories—showed no link between crime and inherited factors.
- A further question is whether environment is a cause of crime and how that can be disentangled from heredity.
- Twin studies and studies on adoptees seem to have reached no firm or satisfactory conclusions.
- It appears that there is a significant difference in IQ between convicted offenders and 'normal' people with the latter eight points higher, but this may be because the less intelligent are more likely to be caught and to confess.
- A number of biochemical factors have been associated with criminal behaviour. These include
  —sexual hormones
  —adrenaline
  —blood sugar
  —cholestorol

—allergies
—vitamins and minerals.

Psychological Positivism

- this form of positivism seeks to find the causes of crime in the mind—Is there a criminal personality?
- behaviour is a function of personality and situation.
- Eysenk considered personality traits were persistent, stable and predictable. He propounded three dimensions of personality: introversion-extroversion (E), neuroticism (N) and psychotism (P). He suggested personalities with a high E, high N, high P would have anti-social tendencies and later attempted to link scores with particular types of offending.
- Sigmund Freud divided personality into the id, the super-ego and the ego. He provided two models of criminal behaviour: mental illness and a weak conscience—a super-ego that has not been adequately socialised.
- The role of upbringing in criminal behaviour is complex and controversial.

Sociological Positivism

- Durkheim considered that society was an actual entity external to individuals that made it up and that crime is a normal part of all healthy societies because of its boundary setting function.
- Environmental criminology goes back at least as far as Quetelet and Guerry and their 'constancy of crime' theory suggesting that some factor other than individual propensity to crime was at work.
- Park proposed that a city was a social super-organism with natural areas parallel with the plant world, the notion of invasion-domination-succession.
- Burgess divided the city into concentric circles (zones) with the area in transition providing the most problems.
- Shaw and McKay by the use of various maps concluded
    — the closer to the centre the greater the problem of delinquency
    — crime rates remained constant despite changes of inhabitants
    — crime problems went hand in hand with other social problems.
  They proposed the notion of 'social disorganization'.

- In the 1970s it was seen that high offender rate areas were not the same as high offence rate areas: the 'rediscovery of the offence' and the importance of the operation of the housing market was noted.
- Wikstrom noted a positive correlation between burglary rates and the percentage of householders with a high annual income.
- Felson propounded the routine activities theory: a burglary requires
  — a likely offender
  — a suitable target
  — an absence of suitable guardians.
- The Brantinghams suggested that most offenders commit crime when criminal opportunities intersect with cognitively known areas.
- Looking at the housing market, Rex and Moore saw the explanation of crime not as lying in the nature of the area itself but in the difficulties experienced by groups obliged to live in it.
- Bottoms compared two similar estates in Sheffield: one had 'tipped' so that there was a 300 per cent difference in recorded crime and he concluded that the housing allocation process was an important factor. In explaining why 'tipping' can happen so quickly Wilson and Kelling produced their 'broken windows' hypothesis: incivilities lead to crime. Skogan supported this: incivilities lead to residents not caring about an area and moving away while others do not wish to move in so the area deteriorates.
- Sparks drew attention to the way that reported figures of crime in general are highly skewed with a high rate of repeated victimisation.

CHAPTER 4

Strain Theories

> Our primary aim lies in discovering how some social structures exert a definite pressure upon certain persons in the society to engage in nonconformist conduct.
>
> Merton (1938)

The American, Robert Merton went from city slum to high fame in academia: it was an irony that this example of the 'American Dream' called that dream into question such that Taylor *et al* (1973) called him 'the cautious rebel'.

His theory of 'anomie' (defined in *Collin's Concise Dictionary* as 'lack of social and moral standards in an individual or society') is out of fashion in some quarters. Whether it should be, the reader must judge.

His starting point was that American statistics—as with those for the UK, showed a higher crime rate among the lower classes than among the upper or monied classes and this is what he sought to explain (this begs the question of undiscovered white collar crime: *Chapter 9*). Merton distinguished *goals* and *means*. All societies have different things that its members believe are worth striving for: in the Western world these are wealth and material possessions. The goals may become so important that the sort of person one is becomes of little importance. If people do not achieve the goals society will look down on them. The accepted means to achieve the goals are through education, hard work and honest toil even if theft and fraud may produce quicker results. What Merton said (and it may not be impossible to draw a parallel with Britain in the 1980s) was that the goals became so important that even dubious means were rewarded with prestige and social status. Winning was the thing, playing the game counted for little. '"Money = success" was the expression coined by Merton as *the* core value of American Society' (Downes and Rock: 1988). The lower classes found the strain the greatest, because their ability to attain the goals was limited by the very structure of society, legitimate opportunities being concentrated in the upper classes. The culture places the emphasis on the goal of wealth and pretends it is available to all, while the social structure limits the possibilities. It is the gap between the culture and the social structure that Merton called *anomie*. Criminal behaviour could be the result of this strain and its accompanying feeling of unfairness.

Most people in America conformed to both the goals and the means. Others, Merton believed, adapted to the strain. His famous typology of deviant adaptions was four-fold:

- *innovators*: these used their own means to attain the goals which could include crime
- *ritualists*: they conformed to the means in an obsessive way and abandoned all hope of reaching the goals, these are the people 'in a rut' and often found in the lower and, indeed, in the middle classes
- *retreatists*: rejected the goals and the means, they are 'in society but not of it' what we would might call 'drop outs', the alcoholics and the tramps; and
- *rebels*: they attempt to substitute their own goals and means.

These types are not totally clear cut; a ritualist may sometimes innovate by small thefts or retreat into alcohol use, for example.

A number of criticisms have been made of Merton's theory. One of the most trenchant is from Laurie Taylor. 'It is as though individuals in society are playing a gigantic fruit machine but the fruit machine is rigged and only some players are constantly rewarded.' He goes on to suggest that the deprived ones use foreign coins (innovators), some give up the game (retreatists), some play on mindlessly (ritualists), while others propose a new game altogether (rebels). Nobody, Taylor writes, asks who put the machine there in the first place or who takes the profits. It is for this reason that the theory is called a 'theory of the middle range': it does not address the aetiology or causes of criminal behaviour. Other critics have pointed out:

- it only addresses utilitarian crimes, it does not explain, e.g. crimes of violence or vandalism
- in real life manual workers do not compare themselves with, for example, medical consultants but only to comparable reference groups
- the theory does not address crimes like business fraud
- it makes no attempt to apply the typologies to women. In this connection Eileen Leonard contends that women's goals are quite different from men's in that they are *relational* rather than *financial*. Financial success is not so important to most women as is marriage and bringing up children. Women's goals are easier to attain and this may partly explain their lower crime rate; and
- it does not explain why a particular deviant adaption is chosen.

Merton's anomie is closely related to the theory of relative deprivation as one of the major causes of crime; one of the cornerstones of what is called the left realist position which we will now look at briefly.

Left realists
Left realists reject any notion that the crime rate is directly controlled by the police. Although this may be the conventional wisdom it is simply

untrue, rather it is the product of four interacting factors, which make up the so called 'square of crime'. These are offenders, victims, the agents of formal control (which includes the police as well as other agencies) and of informal control (the public). The control of crime involves intervention at all the points on the square. They also reject any single factor such as unemployment or poverty as the cause of crime but rather look to relative deprivation. The idea seems to have originated from Runciman (1996) although for him it was essentially a political argument.

- an individual is relatively deprived of X if
- he does not have X
- he sees some other person as having X (notice the subjectivity of this: he may not actually have X)
- he wants X
- he sees no reason why he cannot have X.

It is this apparent injustice that lies at the heart of relative deprivation. In *What is to be Done About Law and Order?* Lea and Young write:

> It is not absolute poverty but poverty experienced as unfair that leads to discontent. The equation is simple: relative deprivation equals discontent: discontent plus a lack of political solution equals crime.

Supporters of the theory point out that:

- it is not limited to explaining working class crime: relative deprivation may be found anywhere in the economic chain
- it is not limited to economic crime: the subculture of violence among the poor and the violence of the better off may be a response to relative deprivation
- it rejects the notion that absolute poverty is a cause of crime because, in the words of Elizabeth Burney, 'most offenders do not lack necessities, rather they crave luxuries'; and
- it provides an explanation for rising crime rates when income and employment are both rising but there is still perceived unfairness.

Chapter 4: Strain Theories—Key Points

- Merton proposed that some social structures exert a pressure upon certain persons to engage in deviant conduct.
- He asked why there was a higher crime rate among the lower classes.
- He distinguished goals (wealth and material possessions) from the means used to obtain them.

- Those goals had become so important that even dubious means bought the rewards.
- The core value of American society was 'Money = Success'.
- The lower classes found that the structure of society made the attainment of wealth difficult even though the culture pretended it was available to all.
- Merton called the gap between culture and social structure 'anomie'.
- Most people conformed to the goals and means while others adapted and the innovators might turn to crime.
- The theory is closely connected to that of relative deprivation: this rejects any single factor like unemployment and poverty as the cause of crime but contends that relative deprivation (seeing that somebody else has something you want and you see no reason why you should not have it) leads to discontent which may in turn lead to crime.

CHAPTER 5

Control Theories

> The predominant criminological theory articulated by chief constables is a conservative variety of 'control theory' . . . attributing rising crime to an erosion of the efficacy of informal controls in the neighbourhood, family and schools.
>
> Robert Reiner (1991)

The essence of control theories is the notion that all people would commit crimes if left to their own devices. 'It is not natural to buy food rather than take food when one sees it, and yet in our society most people buy rather than take' (Williams: 1991). It is the controlling forces, either personal or social, that bring this state of affairs about. Sometimes these forces are too weak and this leaves the individual free to calculate the costs and benefits of crime: there is thus a connection with classical theory.

Some historical perspective is needed to understand control theories. Their history is a long one, stretching back to Hobbes who wrote that it was fear that made men obey society's laws. However, the first modern control theory was that of Albert Reiss in 1951 who drew a distinction between 'personal' and 'social control'. The former involves an acceptance of society's rules of conformity so that they become one's own (what the sociologists call 'internalisation') while the latter involves mere submission to those same rules and relies on social groups and institutions to make them effective. Reiss tested his theory on more than 1,000 young people on probation and found that personal controls were much more important than social controls. The theory owes much to Freud—with those juveniles not accepting society's rules having weak super-egos or consciences.

The concept of a 'stake in conformity' as a mechanism of control was introduced in 1957 by Jackson Toby who proposed that all young people are tempted to break the law but those with more to lose because, for example, they are doing well at school, will not take the risk because their future careers may be adversely affected. He also argued that in a community with a large number of youths with little 'stake in conformity' peer support for deviance results in a high crime rate.

In 1958 Ivan Nye published a study focusing on the family as the single most important source of social control. He referred to four types of social control exercised through the family as:

- direct control: through parents, teachers, police etc
- indirect control: through the conscience or super-ego
- internalised control: through identification with those who influence behaviour, i.e. caring about what other people think of you (what the sociologists call 'significant others'); and
- control through needs satisfaction: which simply means that if all an individual's needs are met there is no point in criminal activity.

Nye came to his conclusions through empirical research involving 780 young people from the state of Washington. He asked them questions about their family life and seven other questions designed to measure delinquent behaviour. One quarter of his sample he called 'most delinquent' and they had the following characteristics:

- complete freedom from parental control or none at all
- large sums of money available to them
- rejection of their parents
- dishonest parents or at least parents who were irritable and difficult to please; and
- mothers who worked outside the home.

Nye's work was severely criticised mainly because his sample contained no youths from large cities and also on the grounds the young people who were most willing to describe their own delinquent activity might be those willing to describe the less desirable aspects of their family life. In addition, the questions designed to measure delinquency contained only two that referred to criminal activity and not all those who criticised were prepared to follow Nye in his extrapolation from these.

In 1961 Walter Reckless propounded his containment theory which he described as a general theory (one that is applicable to all crimes). He described a number of forces that pushed people into crime and those that restrained them. He referred to:

- social pressures: adverse living conditions, family conflicts, lack of opportunities to advance, membership of a minority group
- social pulls: falling in with bad company
- biological pushes: hostility, discontent, boredom, aggressiveness
- external containment: good and supportive family; and
- inner containment: a good 'self concept' feeling that one was of use to society and was law abiding.

However much sense this makes to those reading it some 30 years later, it was heavily criticised because it was difficult to test and because the category where some of the key terms were put seems fairly arbitrary.

Perhaps the name most associated with control theory is that of Travis Hirschi: 'We are all animals and thus naturally capable of committing criminal acts'. Hirschi believed that control was exercised through bonds to social groups and crime occurred when those bonds were weakened or broken. Those bonds were:

- attachment: relationships to people, family, friends, colleagues or to institutions
- commitment: social investment to children, education, job (much like a 'stake in conformity')
- involvement: the person who is busy has no time for crime; and
- beliefs: a belief in society's norms and rules.

Hirschi's theory is based on empirical data from a self-report study (always problematic as this may depend on the subjective interpretation of the questions) in which, among other things, he showed that class and race are only weakly related to offending behaviour. This seeming contradiction with official statistics is worth a slight detour from the central theme.

The British criminologist Stephen Box (1981) believed that this deviation was due to a difference in policy practices and institutional biases. Different stages in the criminal justice system operate in favour of the advantaged and to the detriment of the less favoured, so that, although offending behaviour shows little class and race difference initially a filtering effect within the system itself produces a different end result. In Aaron Cicourel's words, 'What ends up being called justice is negotiable'.

Hirschi's four elements are not written in tablets of stone and Bob Roshier writing in 1989 produced seven:

- affection: most people will avoid criminal behaviour so as not to lose it
- status: again most people will wish not lose the respect of others
- stimulation: most of us would not wish to endanger work or leisure through punishment
- autonomy: again most of us want control of our lives, or at least as much as is possible—and criminal behaviour could mean that we would lose this
- security: comfort and safety is not to be found in prison
- money: we actually need this for some of the other elements and apart from that the effect of a fine is obvious; and
- belief: here we are back to Hirschi.

In 1990 Gottfredson and Hirschi produced *A General Theory of Crime* which they revisited in 1993. It is not possible to do the theory full justice within the confines of an introductory book of this kind, and readers may not be surprised to learn that such a wide-ranging theory has had its critics. It sets out to explain all crimes that result from 'force or fraud in pursuit of self interest'. The authors point out that most crime is trivial, mundane, and requires little planning, skill, or effort—and they link these characteristics to the sort of people likely to indulge in criminal behaviour. The theory has two interdependent aspects described as lack of self-control coupled with opportunity for committing crimes. Lack of self-control is characterised by: lack of diligence, impulsiveness, an inability to postpone gratification, short temper, easy frustration and the taking of risks. People with these attributes will have difficulty, the authors claim, in avoiding the temptation of criminality. These traits remain throughout life and result from ineffective parenting. They do not necessarily appear as criminal behaviour—otherwise the authors would have difficulty in explaining why most crimes are committed by the young—but may appear as heavy smoking, or drinking or a bad work record. In the early form of the theory little attention was paid to opportunity. In 1993 to explain opportunity the authors considered the offence of driving under the influence of alcohol. This clearly requires alcohol and a car. If alcohol consumption is restricted then even if the car is there and the person has low self-control the opportunity is removed by a situational construct.

A number of criticisms have been directed towards the theory: one is that too little attention is paid to the role of the situation; a second is that the theory is tautologous because there is no reason why, in the list of traits characterised by lack of self-control, the authors could not have included a tendency to commit criminal acts and then, of course, there is no theory!

Control theory gains support from work done by Harriet Wilson in a 1978 study of socially deprived families in Birmingham. She devised a 'chaperonage' index attempting to measure the control different families had over their children. Not surprisingly, perhaps, she found that non-delinquent children had parents who accompanied them to school, kept them indoors or under close supervision and knew where they were when they were out. However, in 1980 she was writing that lax parenting was closely associated with severe social handicaps like unemployment and poverty.

Control theory also takes many forms and in 1994 Christie Davies was asking 'Does religion prevent crime?' He showed that the rise in the crime rate corresponded to a decline in church attendance and adherence. He considered that we now live in a society where there is less personal control over individuals who have thus been unleashed in pursuit of immediate gratification, sensation and excitement.

Where stands control theory now? Some writers say that it has gained in popularity, others that it has been neglected because of its unpopularity in liberal sociological circles with its emphasis on discipline and, of course, on control.

I will end with some of the major criticism of the theory. The first is encapsulated in the question 'Yes, but why do they do it?' The theory largely avoids the issue of motivation. It cannot, as Braithwaite (1989) points out, account for the form criminal behaviour takes. It does not tell us why the uncontrolled person turns to heroin use, or becomes a hit man or a price fixing conspirator.

Chapter 5: Control Theories—Key Points

- Control theories are based on the idea that people would commit crimes if left to their own devices and we must seek the forces, either personal or social, that stop them.
- Hobbes believed that it is fear that makes people obey laws.
- Reiss drew a distinction between personal controls that were internalised and stronger than social controls which merely involved submission.
- Toby introduced the 'stake in conformity': some young people had more to lose by criminal activity.
- Nye looked to the family as the source of control.
- The containment theory of Reckless describes a number of forces that push people into crime and those that restrain them.
- Hirschi believed that bonds to social groups exercised control and when these were weakened or broken crime occurred. He also showed that *class* and *race* were only weakly related to crime in spite of the statistics and Box explained that by the way the system filters out the advantaged.
- Gottfredson and Hirschi produced a general theory of crime (and other anti-social behaviour) based on lack of self control (from ineffective parenting) and opportunities.
- Christie Davies believes that the decline in church going had led to a society with less individual control.

CHAPTER 6

Gender, Subcultures, Labelling and Differential Association

By way of an introduction to explanations of deviancy and criminality, this chapter looks at a selection of theories beginning with those revolving around gender differences, subcultures and a theory—which intertwines with several other explanations of offending—known as labelling. The chapter ends with an outline of Sutherland's theory of differential association.

GENDER

> . . . if men behaved like women the courts would be idle and the prisons empty
>
> Wooton (1959)

In 1977 Carol Smart wrote:

> In comparison with the massive documentation on all aspects of male delinquency and criminality, the amount of work carried out in the area of women and crime is extremely limited.[1]

There could be several explanations for this, including:

- women commit fewer crimes so an examination of their crimes is arguably of less interest. In 1992, for example 14 per cent of indictable offences and 22 per cent of summary offences were committed by women;
- the crimes that women do commit tend to be relatively less serious (though not always); and
- criminology itself has tended to have a 'boys own' air about it with most of the studies being by men about men.

In 1950, Otto Pollak challenged the statistics on women's crime. He contended that they were seriously misleading because women's crimes were under recorded. He believed there were two reasons for this:

- in the police, the magistrates' courts and the justice system generally, men dominated and, because they had been taught to be chivalrous, the courts tended to be lenient to female offenders; and

- women were more deceitful than men and so were adept at hiding their crimes. Pollack's evidence for that was their ability to fake orgasms and to conceal menstruation!

However, Farrington and Morris (1983) conducting a study of sentencing in magistrates' courts concluded that the sex of the defendant did not have any direct influence on the severity of the sentence. Women appeared to receive more lenient sentences but this was because they committed less serious offences. However, they did find a difference in the treatment of married and unmarried women. Women in the 'other' category of marital status (unmarried, divorced, but not widowed) received relatively severe sentences. Mary Eaton, in an article which is essentially about bail decisions but has wider relevance, suggests that the court has in its mind a model of the family—male breadwinner and a dependent woman responsible for childcare and domestic labour. She points out that such a model is raised both in mitigation and in reports. Sandra Walklate writes 'The normal family life constructed in the magistrates' court consists of a male and a female in a heterosexual relationship and it is an enduring privileged unit of social responsibility'. The female defendant who falls outside the traditional role is in peril. 'A woman occupying a traditional gender-role is less likely to be subjected to formal social control'. The reason for this is that a woman in that role is involved in a degree of informal social control (Eaton, 1987).

In 1975 Adler, examining the American scene, concluded that one of the results of women's liberation was that not only was female crime rising faster than men's but there was a change in the nature of women's crime which was becoming more like men's. Research in this country has not found any significant statistical support for this. However, the percentage increase of women in prison is growing at a faster rate than for men. This may be because of women apprehended at ports of entry as drug 'mules' and because drug offences tend to attract longer sentences. So why, in general, do women commit less crime? Frances Heidensohn puts forward a three-fold control theory:

- *in the home* a women has limited opportunities for criminality because of the hours spent doing housework and looking after children. Heidensohn describes domesticity as a 'form of detention'.
- many women are reluctant to go into *public places*. One survey found that over half the women in Islington avoided going out after dark. Again this limits opportunities for criminal behaviour. Heidensohn refers to the 'ideology of separate spheres' and this is part of the system that controls women. The traditional view was that 'A women's place is in the home', in other words.

- *at work* most women are supervised by men, are in part-time, often precarious occupations, and are intimidated by various forms of sexual harassment. This is inimical to criminal behaviour in the work-place.

SUBCULTURES

The crucial conditions for the emergence of new social forms is the existence, in effective interaction with one another of a number of actors with similar problems of adjustment.

A Cohen (1955)

Subcultural explanations of delinquency were born in the USA in the 1950s, crossed the Atlantic in the 1960s—although, as we shall see, they did not travel well—were eclipsed by the enthusiasm for labelling theory (see the next section), and arise again, in a neo-Marxist perspective (*Chapter 7*).

Downes and Rock (1988) describe the real gains of subcultural theory as two-fold. First, the most apparently senseless and meaningless forms of aggressive delinquency could be rendered intelligible and rational by taking into account the author's 'definition of the situation'. This means standing in the shoes of the wrongdoer with all his or her ambitions, traditions, aspirations, understandings and beliefs, however different they may be from one's own. Second, delinquency is a solution to the difficulties faced, not a problem.

These theories, like some others outlined in this handbook, concentrate on juvenile delinquency. There are good reasons for this. If juvenile crime can be understood and better still prevented, then there is hope that today's delinquent will not be tomorrow's hardened criminal. In this connection Farrington (1994) tells us that the average age of first offenders is 17.5 years and the average length of a criminal career is 5.8 years. Also, juvenile crime is the fastest area of growth in the criminal statistics.

This is a sound point, though, to dispel the myth of a 'golden age' of young people, Geoffrey Pearson (1994) writes:

A profound historical amnesia has settled round the youth question whereby it is imagined that in the past young people were orderly, disciplined and well behaved.

In fact, the view that 'Children who have been brought up within these 30 years have nothing like the same reverence or submission to their parents . . . This is the chief cause of the increase in crime', was written in 1828 and, in 1939, Morgan was bemoaning '. . . the transplantation of masses of young people to new housing estates where there is little scope for recreation and plenty for mischief . . . the difficulty is intensified by the extension of freedom . . . given to youth in the last generation'.

Before tracing the history of subcultural theories it is necessary to define some of the concepts involved:

- 'culture is all that in human society is socially rather than biologically transmitted' (Marshall, 1994). It is 'the way things are done' and in the dominant culture, we would add, 'by the majority'
- a sub-culture is then a culture within a culture. A subculture is distinct from the dominant culture but its values, norms and behaviours are usually borrowed and recognisable though distorted, exaggerated or even inverted. As an example, we might think of skinheads, whose 'uniform' was an exaggerated version of traditional working-class clothes. Of course, not all sub-cultures are connected to what we would usually consider to be deviancy: anyone who has been present at a dinner in an army officers' mess, for instance, will have been in the presence of a sub-culture; and
- a counter or contra-culture is one in direct opposition to the dominant culture.

In *Delinquent Boys* (1955) Albert Cohen concentrated on gang delinquency. American youths found themselves in a society which offered them little in terms of conventional goals so they developed their own delinquent sub-culture as a solution to their problems. Cohen listed six sub-cultural values that led to crime:

- *non-utilitarianism* Even in cases of theft there seemed no 'profit motive' and the goods would often be discarded or destroyed
- *negativism* The gangs were not just at odds with the dominant culture, they inverted its values (this is sometimes called 'reaction formation', if you know you cannot get something you really want, you demonstrate that you do not care by the pursuit of the opposite)
- *malice* A thread of destructiveness ran through the activities of the gangs
- *short run-hedonism* In Cohen's own words the cult of instant gratification 'reached its finest flower' in these gangs
- *versatility* Theft, violence, vandalism or general hell-raising were all the same; and
- *group autonomy* Gang loyalty came before anything else.

For Cohen, the explanation of this delinquency lay in the nature of democratic schooling; children are made to care about social status and academic achievement and then the system denies these benefits to most of the working class. The delinquent gangs' solution to this was to take the middle class values and turn them upside down, not only to hit back at a system that had let them down but to try and acquire a different sort of status; the 'D stream's revenge' as Cohen described it. They were suffering from 'status frustration' to use his words—and this was the cause of much criminal behaviour.

Although I have described Cohen's work under the heading of *Subcultures* readers may have detected its connection with the strain theory of Merton (*Chapter 4*). Indeed, some writers do not have a separate category for sub-cultures but subsume the topic within strain theory. Merton's theory also concentrates on the utilitarian nature of crime and, indeed, this limitation is one of the criticisms, while Cohen points to its non-utilitarian nature. His theory is close to the rebellion adaption of Merton where the rebellion is against middle class values.

Cloward and Ohlin (1960) tried to resolve this conflict. They produced a four fold classification of lower class youth:

- *Type 1* They strove for middle class membership and economic position
- *Type 2* They strove for middle class membership but not economic position
- *Type 3* They did not strive for middle class membership but did for economic position
- *Type 4* They did not strive for any of the above.

Cohen would have said that *Types 1* and *2* would produce most delinquents because of 'status frustration', but Cloward and Ohlin would contend *Type 3* were the most problematic. They wanted 'fast cars, fancy clothes and swell dames'. If there were no legitimate opportunities for this type to improve their economic status but there were illegitimate opportunities then they would form criminal gangs. If neither sort of opportunity existed then they would form conflict groups and turn to violence out of frustration—these were Cohen's gangs. A final reaction was that of the retreatists who had no legitimate or illegitimate opportunities and did not turn to violence. Their sub-culture led them to drop out into the world of alcohol and drugs.

Various criticisms can be, and have been, levelled at these pioneering ideas and which we ought to consider:

- most working class boys do not suffer status frustration: 'They don't get much but they don't want much either' summarises their world
- the theories do not explain why these youths tend to reform in adulthood although they will still usually be in the same social class
- the theories also fail to explain conformity with the dominant culture, which is the experience of the great majority of young people; and
- they are male biased. In Francis Heidensohn's words, 'Girls, as if some gynocide had struck, are wholly absent'.

In 1957 David Matza and Gresham Sykes argued that:

> much delinquency is based on what is essentially an unrecognised extension of defences to crimes in the form of justifications for deviance that are seen as valid by the delinquent but not by the legal system or society at large.

These justifications are the famous 'techniques of neutralisation' that lie at the heart of Matza's equally famous and attractive 'drift' theory (below). The techniques of neutralisation may be familiar to readers:

- *denial of responsibility* It stems from unloving parents, bad companions, slum neighbourhoods, unfair treatment—all amounting to 'It's not really my fault'. Matza and Sykes call this the 'billiard ball' conception, the person who believes he is helplessly propelled into new situations
- *denial of injury* 'I only borrowed the car' or 'We were only mucking about'
- *denial of the victim* 'The insurance will pay for it' or 'He/she was asking for it'
- *condemnation of the condemners* 'The police, magistrates, politicians, teachers are no better, they are all bent/hypocrites'; and
- *appeal to higher loyalties* The crime was committed to help family or friends—'You can't let your mates down'.

In *Delinquency and Drift* (1964), David Matza pointed to the fact that adolescents are not committed to offending behaviour but drift between that and conventional behaviour. Their initial socialisation taught them not to be deviant and gave them a sense of guilt but they can free themselves from that by using the techniques of neutralisation set out above. Matza coined the term 'subterranean convergence' for the convergence between those techniques and some of the ideologies of the authorities that represented the moral order. Those authorities could themselves excuse criminal behaviour by blaming parents, for example in the same way as the delinquent. He also refers to 'subterranean values', a search for excitement or something different, which exists throughout society. Its respectable members act in accordance with its values in visits to pubs or sporting activities but deviants express these same values in other ways, in the wrong place and time. The simple fact is that for them (and possibly other people, although they resist it) deviancy is fun!

A question that remains is why, given the fact of drift, neutralisation and subterranean values, people indulge in *criminal* behaviour? Matza finds the answer in free-will. He draws a distinction between hard and soft determinism. The former is from the world of positivism (*Chapter 3*), the person wholly controlled by forces outside his control; the second modifies that strict position and suggests a capability to make rational choices but not with complete freedom because of structural constraints.

The delinquent knows what he or she should do and what he or she should not do, but equally knows that he or she may well not be caught: the individual concerned has probably learned some of the necessary skills, like getting into motor cars, from friends. What pushes this kind of person over the line, according to Matza, is a mood of fatalism. They feel powerless, tired of being pushed around, and want to make something happen. Even if caught and appearing in court at least they have the consolation of knowing it is all happening because of them. This restores what Matza describes as 'the mood of humanism'—the individual is *somebody*—but, as he emphasises, delinquency is only an occasional activity.

Matza's theory is attractive for a number of reasons, not least because it feels right. It also shows that the dominant culture does have an influence on delinquents and that the subculture does not demand delinquent behaviour. Both these seem to be reasonable assertions. That said, not all commentators accept the idea of fatalism for which there is no empirical evidence.

Now to the United Kingdom. In 1996 David Downes completed a study of delinquency in the East End of London. He found that offending behaviour was carried out in street corner groups rather than in gangs. He rejected the idea of status frustration but instead found 'dissociation', an opting out from those values that so frustrated Cohen's gang members. He found no evidence of Cloward and Ohlin's groups— but it must be remembered that he was writing at a time of relatively high employment and the retreatist group may now be more in evidence.

In *View from the Boys* (1975), which must be one of the most entertaining books in this field and which repays reading 20 or more years later, Howard Parker wrote about life among boys aged 16 to 19 in 'Roundhouse', an estate in Liverpool.

The boys were not a gang but a loosely knit group. Nevertheless, if you asked the question 'Have you seen any of the boys?' in the right quarters, the question would be understood. They did not form part of a subculture in that parents and children did not hold different views about society. Offending was not the central focus of their lives, although 'knocking off' items was a necessary and integral part of it, and for a time they did rather well out of stealing car radios. The boys were rarely at home, spending most of their time in shops, empty buildings or kicking a football about. Parker refers to a 'social compact' in the estate, where the respectable and the not-so-respectable were tolerant and protective of one another. If the police visited even a respectable household to ask questions about criminal activity they would not be told much.

As outlined under the next heading, labelling theory became the rage in the 1960s and the return of subcultures onto the deviancy stage was marked by Phil Cohen's 1972 paper *Sub-cultural Conflict and Working Class Communities*, a study of 'skinheads'. He pointed to the breakdown of the traditional working class way of life in the East End of London caused by post-war developments, rehousing schemes and immigrant labour. This led to an upwardly mobile suburban working class based on new technologies and a downwardly mobile working class dependant on unskilled manual labour—and it was this latter that the 'skinheads' explored. It was suggested that they were trying to recover traditional working class values and exhibiting in their clothes and behaviour those of their parents. Episodes of 'queer-bashing' and 'paki-bashing' were exaggerated versions of their parents' attitudes to masculinity and immigration.

Much of the new wave of neo-Marxist subcultural work originated from the Centre for Contemporary Cultural Studies at Birmingham University, led by Professor Stuart Hall. Similarly, the greater part of their criticism of earlier American work was based on the fact that it ignored historical and political aspects, by which they largely meant the fundamental problems of capitalism. They suggested that sub-cultural forms are only intended to provide ritualistic, symbolic or magical solutions to the problems posed by the dominant culture. They are symbolic because, in reality, they do nothing about the actual problem. To illustrate this, I consider two books of that period. Paul Willis' *Learning to Labour* (1977) is subtitled *How Working Class Kids Get Working Class Jobs*. Willis noted how the children spent their time 'skiving', 'dossing' and 'having a laff'. They showed no interest in special courses or career advice and anyone who did was an 'ear 'ole' and looked down upon. This counter culture, Willis found as he followed the children into the work place, was very similar to the shop floor culture. School was irrelevant to the problem of the dead end jobs into which they knew they were heading and insubordination was the symbolic solution—which actually solved nothing. 'The solution', Willis wrote, 'ironically is the problem: the boys eventually collude in their own domination'.

In *The Smash Street Kids* (1979) Paul Corrigan introduced an historical dimension into the school situation. He contended that the long fight to win the right to schooling for working class children had been wasted. The system set out to mould them in terms of middle class values. The problem of the irrelevance of the educational system prompted a resistance movement within the school as the magical solution. Part of one of Corrigan's interviews went as follows:

PC: 'What do you do?'
A: 'Sometimes we get into mischief'.
PC: 'Mischief?'
A: 'Well somebody gets a weird idea into their head'
PC: 'Weird idea?'
A: 'They . . . like go around smashing milk bottles'.

Corrigan believes that 'weird ideas' emerge out of the boredom of doing nothing.

LABELLING

Never before had I realised that I was a criminal. I really became one as I sat there and brooded.

Shaw (1966)

The leading commentators whose ideas are usually subsumed under the banner 'labelling theorists' reveal a great divergency of thought and some of them would deny the description/categorisation altogether. Indeed, of all the topics in this book this is the one that is perhaps the most difficult to treat in a succinct manner and at the same time give an adequate account of its varied contributions to thinking about deviance. 'Labelling theory' may also be called 'interactionism' or 'social reaction theory'. It is not just a single, self-contained theory—in fact some people would say that it is not really a coherent theory at all—but a 'perspective whose core problems are the nature, emergence, application and consequences of labels' (Plummer, 1979).

An understanding of labelling requires a passing acquaintance with *phenomenology* and *ethnomethodology*—terminology likely to be off-putting to all but the most enthusiastic reader.

It is possible to perceive labelling theory simply as 'People go about minding their own business and then *wham,* bad society comes along and slaps them with a stigmatising label. Forced into the *role* of deviant, the individual has little choice but *to be* deviant' (Ackers, 1973: emphasis supplied).

We can start our discussion with George Herbert Mead (1863-1931) and his notion of 'self' as socially constructed. A person's self-image is continuously being constructed and re-constructed in interaction with other people with whom that person comes into contact. Mead drew a distinction between 'I' which is essentially subjective and 'me', how we see ourselves as others see us. Human behaviour, Mead believed, could only be understood if this process was borne in mind. Albert Cohen (1966) expresses it thus:

> We cannot really tell whether we are "leaders", "glamour girls", "pool sharks", or "brains" without venturing into the icy waters of social intercourse, trying our hand at the role and seeing how others respond.

I know, from personal experience, that if, for example I am stopped while driving by the police, for the most innocent of reasons, in that initial interaction with the officer my self-image is dented even if it is momentarily: 'I've done something wrong'. It is much worse if someone is wrongly accosted on leaving a store by a security officer and told 'You are a shop-lifter'.

Phenomenology is a philosophical approach which emerged from the debate about the scope and certainty of knowledge. Its essence is captured by Downes and Rock (1988) who urge us to consider a desert: it is not the same to an oil prospector, a painter, a tourist, a Bedouin, a reader *of The Seven Pillars of Wisdom* and neither will it be the same to them at different times. Alfred Schutz (1899-1959) argued that we should not attempt to ascertain the 'reality' of social phenomenon, in just the same way as the desert has no 'reality'. All is subjective.

Phenomenology has had a lasting influence on 'ethnomethodology', a word invented by Garfinkal to describe how people make sense of their everyday social experiences. The main method of ethnomethodology to which I want to refer is 'indexicality'. Any human activity is interpreted differently depending upon the context and viewpoint of the viewer. The circumstances of an incident as seen by the police, witnesses and the defendant might be very different but they might all be telling the 'truth' whatever that is. This comes close to two theories about truth that underpin much sociological writing. The 'correspondence theory of truth' holds that the reality being observed exists independently of the observer while the 'congruence theory of truth' holds that reality is a product of the way observers describe it; so there are multiple realities.

Most of the writers on labelling theory refer to deviance and, of course, criminal behaviour is but one aspect of deviance. In his book *Outsiders,* Howard Becker (1963) explains that if a rule made by a social group is enforced the rule-breaker is seen as a special kind of person, an 'outsider'.

The corollory is that the rule-breaker may have a different rule, he does not accept the rule-enforcer's right to brand him as an outsider. It is they who are outsiders: this is something we see more and more and the drug culture is perhaps one example. Outsiderness (a word I have contrived to use for this purpose) may vary; the motorist who speeds is only mildly an outsider, the true outsider is the murderer and the rapist. Deviance, then, is the failure to obey group rules. Becker carries the argument a significant degree further. Deviance is created by society. Look, e.g. how smoking is rapidly assuming deviant status. In one of the most quoted passages in all of criminology Becker wrote:

> Social groups create deviance by making rules whose infraction constitutes deviance: deviance does not lie in the act itself but rather in the successful application of the label "deviant".

At a somewhat lower level Tierney (1996) refers to Maradonna's 'Hand of God' goal during the 1986 World Cup. The referee did not label it a foul though almost everyone else did. The question is, was it a 'foul'? It was not labelled as such by the man who mattered.

Now we can turn to criminal behaviour and to three important questions:

- why are some acts labelled 'criminal'?
- who is likely to be labelled criminal and who not?
- what is the effect on a person of being so labelled?

Most people probably think of crime as unproblematic. Some acts are crimes, some are not. But a moment's thought will show that this is not nearly so clear. A few years ago insider dealing was shrewd business, now it's a crime. The very same drugs that were freely available to treat childrens' ailments early in this century are now 'controlled drugs'. So there are changes across time but more than that the same act is not always a crime. Becker's own example was the injection of heroin into a vein. Perfectly proper if done by a nurse under a doctor's instruction but, when not publicly defined as proper, the act is criminal. Even the killing of another human being is not always murder. Pfohl (1985) draws a comparison between killing by a police officer and killing of a police officer, between stabbing an old lady in the back and doing the same to an enemy in wartime. What is criminal is simply behaviour that people so label. High spirits by undergraduates may well be the affray of working class youths. This leads us into the second question above. Again the answer seems obvious, it is those who break the criminal law who are labelled as criminals. But as we know only too well the innocent may be imprisoned and labelled and many of those who break the law never enter the criminal justice system at all.

Interesting work was carried out by the Americans, Piliavin and Briar (1964) who showed that actual behaviour was only one factor in deciding whether a criminal label should be affixed to an individual. They contended that, so far as the police were concerned, there were non-legal factors which influenced the arrest decision. There were certain 'cues' by which officers labelled youths. There were various personal factors, including appearance, demeanour, dress—and structural factors, class, the area in which the person was at the time of the events in question and the time of day. If a youth was stopped and was demure and respectful he was more likely to be sent on his way than if he were rude and uncooperative.

Whether the same notions can be applied in Britain is a vexed question with no conclusive answer. For example, there is a consistent body of evidence to suggest that African-Caribbeans are more likely to be stopped and searched by the police: Willis (1983) says two or three times as likely. Other studies have not indicated any police prejudice although certainly young people are stopped more and a disproportionate number of young people are from ethnic minorities.

And what of the consequences of being labelled deviant? In his 1927 study of gangs in Chicago, Thrasher postulated that these gangs had begun as little more than street play groups but as they had grown older they were perceived as gangs by people in the neighbourhood and this had such a negative effect that they then began to behave as a gang.

An early labelling theorist was Tannenbaum, often described as the father of labelling. His 1936 'dramatisation of evil' theory was the foundation of much later work. He believed that if the *actions* of an individual were seen as evil, then the next step was for the *individual* to be seen as evil. He or she would be 'tagged', the word Tannenbaum used in place of 'labelled', and this would lead to his or her isolation. He or she would perceive themselves as 'criminal', particularly if sent to prison. The process of public labelling as criminal was crucial in the making of a criminal. 'The person becomes the thing he is described as being'.

In 1951 Edwin Lemert, another architect of labelling, drew a distinction between *primary* and *secondary* deviance. With primary deviance the wrongdoer does not see himself or herself as criminal; he or she is only taking a few tools from work and everybody does it, so self-image is not effected. But if there is a social reaction to whatever has been done because, for example the police have discovered it, then he or she may become a secondary deviant. This may happen after one transgression or a number but, particularly if wrongdoing becomes known to that part of society significant to the perpetrator—colleagues, family, or parents perhaps—then he or she will internalise the label 'criminal'. It will become, what sociologists call his or her 'master status' displacing 'parent' or 'worker' or whatever. If he or she is sent to prison things will be worse. The individual will be cut off from friends, associate with other law breakers, find it difficult to get into work on release and the police will assuredly keep an eye on him or her. Prison provides a strong case for the labelling theorists.

Moving away from crime for a moment, as Young (1995), points out Lemert is particularly convincing in his research on *Stuttering Among the North Pacific Coastal Indians*. Some tribes paid particular attention to singing, dancing and speech making. The children were expected to become competent and the tribe showed great sensitivity to speech defects. They had a word for 'stuttering' and those who suffered were likely to be treated as outcasts. Other tribes were not concerned about stuttering and had no word for it; stuttering was unknown. The conclusion is that it is concern about stuttering that actually produces it and that we will link to deviant behaviour in groups later.

Labelling theory has had a profound effect on criminology but is not without strong critics. Gibbs (1966) has pointed out that though labelling may have some effect on some deviance this does not apply in the case of hard deviants. Everyone realises that some crimes are bad in themselves: they are fully aware that murder, for example is criminal and labelling is then irrelevant. Neither do the theories explain the reasons for primary deviation (above).

Labelling theories are excessively deterministic: given certain factors there will be a certain outcome and the actor cannot avoid it, what Gouldner calls the 'man on his back' rather than the 'man fighting back'. They overlook the victim and take the side of the deviant. Becker thought that this was no bad thing and in *Whose Side Are We On?* (1967) pleaded for a redressing of the balance. Empirical testing of the theories is lacking.

Labelling theories have had an impact on the criminal justice system. The attempts to keep people away from the system through diversion is a logical extension of labelling theory—in that if someone does not go to prison they are not tarred with being a prisoner or ex-prisoner. We see this in the idea of cautioning (now set to become warnings and reprimands) and in the movement towards decarceration of people committing less serious offence via statutory restrictions on imprisonment. These diversions from custody include community service orders, probation and combination orders. Some commentators, like Stanley Cohen, are unhappy with these community orders because they involve an even deeper intrusion into peoples' lives, like the new probation orders (what he calls 'thinning the mesh') and effect more people (those who would have been fined are now punished in the community: 'net-widening' as he and others describe it). All this, of course, without any actual reduction in the prison population (and at the time of writing quite substantial annual increases). Eventually, Cohen believes 'It will be impossible to determine who exactly is enmeshed in the social control system'. Perhaps the answer to that is, all of us.

On a more optimistic note, John Braithwaite (1989), whose theory of 'reintegrative shaming' (*Chapter 8*) is very much linked to labelling theories wrote that 'Societies with low crime rates are those that shame potently and judiciously'. Wrongdoers should be shamed not to stigmatise them (labelling) but to encourage them back into society. This kind of thinking is also behind the idea of reparation, when the offender faces up to his or her victim.

The notion of restorative justice is being much discussed at present. It is underpinned by the idea that if punishment does not prevent crime then we should look elsewhere. Redress or restoration is a more progressive policy than punishment. There seem to be two difficulties:

- it is perhaps too easy to assume that it will be possible to reach an agreement satisfying the three parties: offender, victim and community; and
- if only certain more serious crimes were to be dealt with by the criminal law the victims to whom the restorative process applied would feel that their troubles were of lesser importance. This fragmentation of the criminal justice system would be bound to bring in its wake many problems.

Labelling theory can be applied at a group rather than at an individual level. This point is reflected in the work of Leslie Wilkins (1964) whose 'deviancy amplification' theory suggests that a small initial deviation may spiral into ever increasing significance through labelling and over reaction. One group labels another 'deviant', that leads to more crime in the latter group arising from their social exclusion. This justifies the original group's reaction and so deviancy amplification leads to a spiral of crime. It is now generally acknowledged that something similar to this arose from 'Operation Swamp' in Brixton in 1981 (see the Scarman Report: *The Brixton Disorders 10-12 April 1981*, HMSO, Cmnd. 8427, 1981). The stopping and searching of black youths by police officers drafted in, in great numbers, actually led to the very crimes that it was intended to avoid.

In another context, O Gill (1977) describes in *Luke Street* how a council accommodated what it classified as 'problem families' in one small area of Merseyside. Employment was withheld from those in the area, and any delinquency in that area, however minor, received wide press coverage. The police harassed the families, the young people were banned from youth clubs and the result was inevitable: a 'running battle' with the police.

A further example comes from Stanley Cohen's work *Folk Devils and Moral Panics* written in 1973, and ostensibly about the 'mods and rockers' although the applications are wider. Essentially the press were guilty of exaggeration about events on a wet, cold, bank holiday weekend in Clacton in 1964. Increased public concern led to an increased police response, and this led to more arrests which justified the public's concern, leading to greater pressure on the police. This resulted in whole towns on the south coast 'holding their breath'. The fact that subsequently nothing happened was not reported. The 'mods and rockers' had become folk devils. We have seen a few of these in recent years ranging from dangerous dogs to Jamaican yardies drug dealers.

DIFFERENTIAL ASSOCIATION

Further theories which command substantial exposition in their own right are discussed in the next chapter. However, one further, if now less mainstream and popular—though nonetheless significant—theory which it seems convenient to mention here is Sutherland's explanation of criminality and deviance.

> I reached the general conclusion that a concrete condition cannot be a cause of crime . . . it seemed to me that learning, interaction and communication were the processes around which a theory of criminal behaviour should be developed.
>
> Edwin Sutherland

Most behaviours have to be learned: why not criminal behaviours? The major learning theory is that of Edwin Sutherland (1883-1950) and his notion of 'differential association'.

However, before Sutherland came Gabriel Tarde (1843-1904), an important figure because of his rejection of Lombroso's theory (see, generally, *Chapter 3*) who argued that criminals were normal people who had the misfortune to be brought up where they learned criminal behaviour as a way of life. His theory is known as 'Tarde's laws of imitation': his first law, the most important for our present purpose, is that people imitate each other in proportion to how much close contact they have with one another.

Sutherland's theory was briefly stated in 1934, more formally presented in 1939 and expanded on in 1947. I will examine the theory in its final form. It is best summarised as a number of points to which can be added brief comments:

- criminal behaviour is learned in interaction with other people in small intimate personal groups in a process of communication. It can be noted that this omits any learning from books, magazines, television and films—and it is not a universally held view today. In particular, Albert Bandura (1986) strongly believes in the influence of television as a source of observational learning of crimes against the person.
- what is learned includes the techniques for committing the crime and the specific direction of motive, drives, rationalisations and attitudes. This second limb simply means 'why' the crime is committed.
- the specific direction of motives and drives is learned from definitions of legal codes as favourable and unfavourable. This derives from the symbolic interactionism of Mead, who I have already mentioned (see p.61). Experiences in someone's life like, for example, unemployment or a learning difficulty, will mean different things to different people. We have all read stories based on the plot of two brothers brought up in the same poor circumstances. One becomes an Archbishop and the other a Mafia boss, or something just as unlikely. Out of those experiences people derive definitions but then generalise them so that they become a way of looking at things. Two people may then react to a similar situation in different ways through this process of experience, meaning, generalisation, reaction. These definitions are learned in a normal learning process and whether people violate the law depends on how they define the conditions they experience
- an individual becomes delinquent because of an excess of definitions favourable to violations of the law over definitions unfavourable to violation of the law: the principle of differential association
- differential association may vary in frequency, duration, priority, and intensity. Sutherland argues that the longer someone is exposed to definitions favourable to law violations the more likely are violations, and this also varies with the prestige of the person from whom the person is learning and how early in life is the experience
- criminal behaviour and non-criminal behaviour are expressions of the same needs and values. Thieves generally steal in order to secure money but likewise honest labourers work in order to do the same. He goes on to make the point that it is futile to attempt to explain criminal behaviour in terms of striving for social status, the money motive and frustration—because these explain lawful behaviour just as completely.

The theory, although influential, has had its share of criticisms, among these that:

- it does not explain impulsive, opportunistic crimes
- people commit crimes who have had no contact with criminals
- it is largely a deterministic theory, if a person has more of one sort of definition poured into him or her than another, he or she will indulge in criminal behaviour ; and
- we are not really told what these definitions, that Sutherland makes so much of, actually are.

The theory received support from a rather unusual source in 1987 in research by James Orcutt (quoted in Wayne Morrison, 1995). Orcutt divided a group of college students according to their definitions of marijuana use into positive, negative and neutral. He then ascertained how many of each student's four closest friends smoked at least once a month. Those with a positive response smoked if at least one of those friends was a semi-regular user, those with a negative attitude avoided smoking whatever the friends did. In the case of those with a neutral attitude the chances of them smoking were zero if none of their closest friends did, 1:4 in cases where one was a regular user, and 1:2 where two or more were regular users.

Since Sutherland first published his theory of differential association others have modified it. Glaser (1956), for example thought that learning was not based on association between individuals but involved identifying with a criminal role and a desire to emulate it. There was no need for a meeting: the media was influence enough.

We should note that Sutherland originally expounded his theory to explain white collar crime (*Chapter 9*). The idea is that when businessmen learn 'the realities of business' they become willing to commit crimes to enhance the company although they would never contemplate crime on their own behalf.

Chapter 5: Gender, Subcultures, Labelling and Differential Association—Key Points

Gender

- Relatively little work has been done on women and crime in the overall scheme of criminology, perhaps because their crimes are fewer, tend to be less serious and largely speaking criminology practitioners have been men studying men.

- Pollock challenged the statistics which he thought misleading because of male chivalry and because women, he claimed, were adept at hiding their crimes.
- Farrington and Morris found that sex does not directly influence sentencing but that women who fill traditional roles were treated more leniently.
- The reasons given by Heidensohn for women committing less crime were the importance of home where there were less opportunities to offend, a reluctance to go into public places and part-time precarious work.

Subcultures

- According to Downes and Rock the advantages of subcultural theory as an explanation for delinquency lie in the 'definition of the situation': events will be seen from various points of view— and 'delinquency is the solution not the problem'.
- Pearson has dispelled the myth of a 'golden age' of young people.
- Marshall defines 'culture' as all that is transmitted socially rather than biologically.
- A sub-culture is a culture within a culture.
- Albert Cohen found the explanation for delinquency in 'status frustration'.
- Cloward and Ohlin considered that it was those who strived for economic position rather than those who suffered 'status frustration' who were most likely to be delinquent.
- The drift theory of Matza has as its heart the techniques of neutralisation and free-will connected with soft determinism.
- Downes found no 'status frustration' in the UK but 'dissociation' an opting out.
- Phil Cohen found that 'skinheads' were trying to recover working class values and exaggerating their parents' attitudes.
- Both Willis and Corrigan examined the school situation and found that subcultural forms provided only symbolic solutions to problems posed by the dominant culture.

Labelling

- Labelling is a perspective on labels rather than a self-contained theory.
- Mead saw a person's self-image as constantly changing in interaction with other people.
- Phenomenology suggests that social phenomena have no reality and points to the importance of the subjective.

- The main method of ethnomethodology is 'indexicality'—any human activity is interpreted differently depending on the viewpoint and each may be true.
- Becker argues that deviance lies not in the act itself but in society's reaction so that deviance is created by society.
- What is criminal is any act that people so label.
- Tannenbaum, the 'father of labelling', in his 'dramatisation of evil' theory argued that if *the actions* of a person were seen as evil the next step was for *the person* to be 'tagged' as evil and so perceive himself or herself as criminal.
- Lemert drew a distinction between *primary* deviance (the wrongdoer does not see himself as a criminal) and *secondary* deviance (a social reaction to what he has done affects his self-image and he internalises the label 'criminal').
- Although labelling has had its critics it has had an impact on the criminal justice system as illustrated by diversion strategies.
- Braithwaite, in his theory of reintegrative shaming, proposed that wrongdoers should be shamed to encourage them back into society not stigmatised (labelled).
- Wilkins calls the labelling of a group rather than an individual deviancy amplification, for example Operation Swamp and the 'mods and rockers'.

Differential Association

- In his law of imitation Tarde suggested that people imitate each other in proportion to their close contact.
- In the theory of differential association Sutherland said that criminal behaviour and its methods is learned in interaction with other people in small groups and through a process of communication.
- It is an excess of definitions favourable to law breaking over definitions that are unfavourable that constitutes 'differential association'.
- Glaser did not agree that a meeting was required but only an identification with a criminal role and a wish to emulate it.

---

[1] Indeed, women are often an invisible component of criminology and criminal justice, many aspects of the latter not having been designed to take account of women's different needs: see, for example, *Invisible Women: What's Wrong With Women's Prisons?*, Angela Devlin, Waterside Press, 1998. As that work was published the Prison Department appointed a woman director with special responsibility for female establishments.

CHAPTER 7

Conflict and Radical Criminology

> No more laws! No more judges! Freedom, Brotherhood . . . are the only
> effective bulwark we can raise to the anti-social instincts of a few among us.
>
> Peter Kropotkin, 1898

Criminologists who adhere to a *critical* or *radical* view see the causes of crime in social conflict and the power of some people to develop laws and enforce them against others. The division between the two is subtle or indistinct, but it is generally accepted that the *critical* approach will concede that adjustments to the capitalist system are all that is required while the *radical* approach, with a strong Marxist or, at least, neo-Marxist influence, would seek to replace the whole system.

MARXIST AND RADICAL PERSPECTIVES

Many of the writers mentioned in this chapter are American but two British authors writing in the 1950s considered the confrontation between working class values and the authorities. John Mays (1954) thought that lower class culture was not *intentionally criminal* but simply *different*—and that the culture's beliefs just happened to clash with many legal rules. Terence Morris (1957) believed that anti-social behaviour of some sort existed throughout all classes but that the working class expression happened to be through criminal behaviour. Initially I shall examine this topic through the work of a number of other authors.

William Bonger
Bonger was the standard bearer of Marxist orthodoxy and believed in a causal link between crime and economic social conditions. He asked from whence does the 'criminal thought' arise? In more primitive societies, he thought, altruism ruled behaviour—but once a system of exchange arose—and capitalism is that system writ large—then self-interest would create egoism which would produce a favourable climate for criminal action. The poor would commit crime either out of need or from a sense of injustice and the rich to protect their business interests. 'Capitalism', Bonger wrote, 'has developed egoism at the expense of altruism'.

Thorsten Sellin
Sellin examined culture conflict. His view was that in a healthy homogenous society the rules of behaviour, or norms, became laws and

were upheld by that society. Conflict could occur when separate cultures had their own norms. He separated primary conflicts from secondary conflicts. The former could occur in three situations:

- what he called 'border conflict' when the two culture were close together
- when one culture crossed into the other and tried to extend its power; and
- when one crossed into another and the host culture attempted to dominate.

It perhaps hardly needs explaining that this is the situation we see with regard to immigration.

Secondary conflict occurred where there was one culture but within it a subculture with its own norms which by living within its own rules was breaking the rules of the other. This is not the situation described by Cohen or Cloward and Ohlin (see *Chapter 6*) and has nothing to do with middle-class values. In this present case the norms of the two cultures are intrinsically different.

George Vold

Vold's theory is about conflict between interest groups in the same culture. People are naturally group orientated and may come together to form a group to push for their particular interests in the political arena. This is epitomised in the phrase 'There ought to be a law against it'. There will then be two groups with conflicting interests (as with fox hunting or genetically modified foods, for example) and they may reach a compromise, or one may be able to persuade the state to enforce its interests when the losing group will be on the wrong side of the law. The theory is interesting but only of limited application because much criminal behaviour does not arise out of group or sectional interests.

Austin Turk

Turk's arguments are wide ranging, sophisticated and stimulating (and I thus regret having to deal with these so briefly). It was Turk, who in his autobiography, wrote:

> . . . I learned that life is neither easy nor just for most folks . . . that access to resources and opportunities have no necessary association with ability or character: that the meaning of justice in theory is debatable, and of justice in practice manipulable . . .

His students, he tells us 'were especially bothered about the unreality of criminological studies' and it was this he tried to address.

Turk considered that some conflict in society was healthy but not too much because a society needs a degree of consensus, and not too little because that means there is too much control or too much consensus. He was particularly interested in how conflict arose between the authorities and subjects. He distinguished cultural norms which set out what behaviour is expected, from social norms which is what the behaviour is in practice. From the point of view of the authorities the cultural norms are the laws that have been enacted and the social norms their enforcement, while as far as the subjects are concerned they are their beliefs and behaviours.

If the cultural norms and the social norms correspond—and so do the beliefs and behaviours of the subjects—there *is no* conflict; but, if they differ, there *is* conflict. To take an example, if the law forbids the possession of a certain drug and the police rigorously enforce the law and the subjects believe it should be banned and don't use it, there will be no conflict. On the other hand, if the subjects believe it should be freely available and use it, then there will be conflict. If, of course, the police do not enforce a law, as seems to be the case in some areas with 'soft drugs', there is less likelihood of conflict.

Turk also makes an interesting point about the situation where law enforcement agencies have different views. He refers to first-line enforcers, like the police, trading standards officers and TV licence inspectors and higher-level enforcers such as judges or magistrates. If both first-line enforcers and the higher-level enforcers are strongly committed to the 'criminality' of the particular behaviour then there will be many arrests, many convictions and severe sentences will be passed. However, for example if the first-line enforcers are not enthusiastic but the high-level enforcers are, there will be few arrests—but those arrested are likely to be convicted and sentenced severely. The importance of this is that it shows that criminality may not, perhaps, be as clear cut as we had imagined and that it is dependant on many factors.

Richard Quinney

Quinney's outlook has changed over time but in his 1970 theory of the 'social reality of crime' he expressed six propositions which I will attempt to summarise.

Crime is a definition of human conduct created by authorised agents and that definition describes behaviours that conflict with the interests of those segments of society with the power to shape and enforce the criminal law. Once an offence has been created and before it becomes a 'social reality' it needs to be communicated to society. What Quinney means, I believe, is that after an offence has become a social reality its purpose and, indeed, its logic is forgotten and it becomes a 'social given'. He continues: 'The social reality of crime in a politically organized society is constructed as a political act'. This argument is all very well, but the fact is that the law does protect all individuals and not only the powerful.

William Chambliss
Chambliss' views are an example of a radical perspective. He contended that acts defined as criminal were to protect the economic ruling class and part of the purpose of creating crime was to reduce surplus labour by providing jobs in, for example law enforcement. He also considered that crime diverted the attention of the working class from the way that the capitalist system exploited them by turning their attention to the criminal tendencies of their own class.

United Kindom commentators
It is now time to consider what had been happening on this side of the world. In 1973, Ian Taylor, Paul Walton and Jock Young published *The New Criminology* which suggested that the freedom and non-oppressive nature of a socialist order would enable a non-aggressive society to flourish. They did seem to believe that the abolition of crime was a real possibility under a socialist order. Of course, since then we have seen the collapse of the communist system in Europe and many of its failings are now better revealed and understood. Jock Young has 'jumped ship' and as the leading proponent of left realism has been much criticised for his desertion as he explains in *What Is to be Done About Law and Order?* (1983).

Another work which was something of a milestone at this time came from the Birmingham School (also mentioned at p.59). This was *Policing the Crisis* by Stuart Hall *et al*, published some 20 years ago. Although some people may disagree with much of the book, it is still worth reading: it is largely an exposition of 'mugging', a term imported from the USA and unknown in our legislation (although robbery which *ex hypothesi* involves theft, violence and fear has been around a long time). The government of the day reported on a frightening rise in 'street crime', largely due to the prevalence of mugging which, it was reported, had increased in London, by 129 per cent between 1968 and 1972. Hall *et al* contended that this figure (and strangely there were no comparable figures for the provinces available) was an invention and arrived at by conflating different crimes. When the official reaction to a person, group of persons or a series of events is out of all proportion to the actual threat—it is appropriate to speak of a 'moral panic'. But why?

To explain this phenomenon I will turn for a moment to Antonio Gramsci, the Italian Marxist who suggested that when the ruling bloc in a society maintains its control and supremacy with the approval and consent of the governed then this is 'hegemony'. In the 1950s in Britain there was a consensus and little public disorder but, in the 1970s, there was greater public dissent—Northern Ireland, student militancy and widespread strikes all led to a 'crisis of authority'. In response to this the government's war against crime became a source of its re-legitimation. In the crisis, deviants, criminals, industrial dissidents and scroungers were all seen as part of the problem by the state. It was not the capitalist system that was at fault it was 'the enemy within'. The working class were persuaded to misrecognise the enemy. The main scapegoat for society's ills, the folk devil *par excellence*, was the black mugger! Policing the blacks became policing the crisis.

Most writers now agree that Hall's case is flawed. P. Waddington (1986), for example showed that there was a real and continuous national rise in muggings before the moral panic.

THE 'NEW RIGHT'

Radical criminology is not confined to the left of the political spectrum and I must now deal briefly with the New Right and try to give a flavour of the views encompassed by this term. As Tame (1993) explains, the commentators come from a variety of standpoints: libertarians, economists, conservatives and New Realists. If they have a banner under which they could all fight it is, freedom, justice and responsibility.

The libertarians would contend that individual freedom should only be limited by the duty not to initiate force against others. They, reject 'victimless crimes' which 'do not violate people's rights: drunkenness, possession of drugs, prostitution, homosexuality, vagrancy, loitering, the product of pornography, and the like' (Wollstein, 1967). They believe that the rejection of the idea of individual responsibility and free will has led to an unwillingness 'to shoulder the responsibility for punishing [those] who deprive other individuals of their life, liberty and property'. (Szasz ,1997)

One of their number argues that the 'crime explosion' is primarily a result of the 'excuse-making industry', among whom he numbers sociologists and criminologists! (Bidinotto, 1989).

The economic liberals have revived as part of the revival of classical free market economics. To them it is not capitalism that is the cause of crime but collectivism. Christie Davies (1983) sees the eclipse of law-abiding Britain as being traceable to:

> the ever-increasing bureaucratic centralization of British society in the twentieth century and the linked, but independent, rise of a corrosive ethic of socialist egalitarianism.

The traditional conservatives have similarities with the libertarians. Ernest van den Haag vigorously defends capital punishment. Its abolition is:

> . . . perceived symbolically as a loss of nerve: social authority is no longer willing to pass an irrevocable judgement on anyone. Murder is no longer thought grave enough to take the murderer's life. Respect for life itself is diminished as the price for taking it is. Life becomes cheaper as we become kinder to those who wantonly take it (van der Haag 1975).

Rosemary Morgan (1978) expresses surprise that many sociologists and criminologists seem to view crime as revolutionary expressions of the working class when it is members of that class who suffer the most.

The new realists' view can perhaps be encapsulated in the writings of Stanton Samenow (1984):

> . . . criminals choose to commit crimes. Crimes reside within the person and are 'caused' by the way he thinks, not by his environment . . . Criminals cause crime—not bad neighbourhoods, inadequate parents, television, schools, drugs or unemployment. Crime resides within the mind of human beings and is not caused by social conditions.

(Quotations in this section are from Tame, 1993)

• • •

Chapter 7: Conflict/Radical Criminology—Key Points

- Critical and radical criminologists see the causes of crime in social conflict and power differences.
- Critical criminologists accept that adjustments to the capitalist system will suffice.
- Radical criminologists seek to replace the capitalist system.
- Bonger considered that the 'criminal thought' arose out of the way in which the capitalist system developed egoism at the expense of altruism.
- Sellin found conflict in cultures either in primary conflict (two cultures) or secondary conflict (one culture but a subculture within whose norms conflicted).
- Vold found conflict in interest groups particularly when the state enforced the interests of one group but not the other.
- Turk thought some conflict was healthy but not too much or too little. Conflict arose between authorities and subjects and he

distinguished cultural norms (expected behaviour) and social norms (behaviour in practice). There could also be conflict between first line enforcers and higher level enforcers about some acts.

- Quinney believed that when an offence became a 'social reality' and its original purpose and logic was forgotten: it was a social given and constructed as a political act.
- Chambliss considered that acts were defined as criminal to protect the economic ruling class and also to divert the attention of the working class.
- In *Policing the Crisis* it was suggested that scapegoating the black mugger was used by the state as a method of re-legitimation after hegemony had been replaced by a crisis in authority.
- Radical criminology from the right of the political spectrum has a number of standpoints but in common are freedom, justice and responsibility.

CHAPTER 8

Victimology, Fear of Crime, Restorative Justice—and a Look at Some Statistics

Studying victims has become one of the growth industries of criminology.

Zedner (1994)

The seminal text on victimology is Von Hentig's *The Criminal and His Victim* (1948) where the author criticises criminology for being *offender* orientated and proposes a more interactionist stance in place of the usual one of considering the victim simply as a passive actor. 'We meet a victim who consents tacitly, co-operates, conspires or provokes', he wrote, 'in a considerable number of cases'. He produced a typology of victims and suggested that some people were 'victim prone'.

Mendelsohn (1956) tried to discover those personal characteristics which made some people more susceptible to victimisation than others. His typology of victims ranged from the 'completely innocent' to the 'most guilty' victims. In *Patterns in Criminal Homicide* (1958), Wolfgang defined victim-precipitated offences as those 'in which the victim is a direct positive precipitator in the crime'. Working from police records in Philadelphia he calculated that over a quarter of homicides resulted from violence initiated by the victim. Then came Amir's controversial *Patterns of Forcible Rape* (1971) where the author suggested that nearly one-fifth of rapes were victim precipitated. His definition of precipitation included situations where :

- the victim agreed to have sexual relations but retracted; or
- did not resist strongly enough; or
- entered vulnerable situations charged sexually.

Not surprisingly, the newly emergent feminist movement was highly critical of this approach.

One point of this broad overview of some of the literature concerning victims is that it illustrates how victim *proneness* becomes victim *precipitation* which so easily then becomes victim *blaming*, and this has bedevilled what might be called 'old victimology'. If readers think that this is no longer applicable in modern, more enlightened times I would remind them of Judge Richards who said, in 1982, 'It is the height of imprudence for any girl to hitch-hike at night . . . She is in the true sense asking for it'. Similar comments have been made by judges even more recently.

Some writers have defended the concept of victim precipitation and contended that it need not mean victim blaming; others consider that it is difficult to shed the blame element from it. Perhaps, with Miers (1989) we might agree that *some* victims bear *some* responsibility for *some* crimes.

Sandra Walklate (1995), who has written extensively on this topic, and to whom I will refer again later, has expressed a fear that the great trinity of positivism, determinism (human behaviour is not rationally chosen), differentiation (criminals are different from non-criminals), and pathology (not only different but abnormal) could become a way of thinking about victims. Just as there is a 'normal' person and a criminal falls short of that 'normality', so too, in some ways, does a victim.

STATISTICS AND CRIME

What turned criminology from its concentration on offenders rather than victims was the development of the victim survey. Here I will turn aside from my main theme and look briefly at the vexed question of statistics of crime.

The 'Official Statistics' are collated from returns from the police, and this immediately creates problems. They are statistics '. . . collected not by agencies designed to collect statistics but by agencies designed to enforce the law' (Wiles, 1991). This suggests that statistics tell us more about the institution collecting the statistics than about crime itself.

Nevertheless these figures suggest an enormous increase in crime, from about one and a half million crimes per annum in 1970 to five and a half million in 1992, after which there has been a slight decrease overall—although recorded violent crime has been rising steadily. But again we must be careful how we use these figures. The population of the UK has grown, so more crime can be expected; perhaps less obvious as a factor is the increase in the number of police and their supporting apparatus and technology. The growth in the number of private telephones making the reporting of crime easier is another factor; and so too are shifts in public attitudes and tolerance. There has been an increase in crime, of that there is no doubt, but there are all sorts of reasons for the figures apart from the 'real' increase.

Well over 90 per cent of crime comes to the notice of the police from reports made by members of the public and that process is more problematic than it may seem:

- a member of the public must first know of the crime
- that person must then define the act as a crime. Crimes are, as the sociologists say, 'social constructs'. They do not have some

separate existence apart from society and its view of them. An 'assault' is unproblematic until you watch a football match with a bit of tension in it, when there will be a number of 'assaults' which no one would report as a crime. Some 'thefts' from work are seen as perks rather than crimes, both by employees and employers unless they get out of hand (see also *White Collar Crime, Chapter 9*)

- the crime must then be reported to the police and there are plenty of reasons why that may not happen, for example it may be too trivial, people may not want 'to get involved' or tell on a mate and so on; and

- to appear in the statistics, the police must then record the event as a crime. There are reasons why this may not happen—some quite dubious. It may be a mistake (the 'stolen' bicycle was mislaid) or the complainant may not wish to proceed. Other reasons may be rather different. Bottomley and Coleman (1981) refer to the process of 'cuffing' where, if there seems little chance of the crime being cleared up, it is simply not recorded to save unwelcome paperwork and, if done often enough, to improve the clear up rate. This difference between reported and recorded crime is referred to by Bottomley and Pease (1986) as the 'grey figure' and it has been suggested that it may be that as much as 40 per cent of crimes reported are not recorded. In 1977, Sparks *et al* showed in a study of three London boroughs that the proportion of incidents *reported* by victims was lowest in Brixton and highest in Kensington—and the proportion *recorded* was highest in Kensington and lowest in Hackney, even lower than in Brixton. The whole question of police discretion is well illustrated by Farrington and Dowds (1985) and their research in Nottinghamshire. That county showed the highest serious crime rate in England and Wales, which seemed unlikely in fact. The authors discovered that 25 per cent of all crimes came to light when offenders admitted them, whereas the figure in neighbouring Leicestershire, which had a different policy, was four per cent. There was also a greater tendency for trivial offences to be recorded in Nottinghamshire. Although the Home Office has sought to remove inconsistencies—for example forces are now precluded from recording as 'detected' crimes admitted by those serving custodial sentences—it remains true that to understand statistics one must understand what happens in police stations.

The process whereby an act has a number of hurdles at which it may fall before it becomes a statistic is known as 'attrition'. It seems that for a range of offences, including theft and criminal damage, only some two or three per cent of offences which occur actually result in a successful prosecution.

For many years criminologists have been concerned about the so-called 'dark figure', the difference between the number of crimes actually committed and the number reported. This was one reason for the *British Crime Survey* (BCS) carried out by the Home Office Research and Planning Unit, in 1982, 1988, 1990, 1992, 1994 and 1998—with an intention that further surveys should be done at two yearly intervals. The figures are collected from face-to-face interviews in over 10,000 households and there are both general and specific questions. These latter questions have dealt with such matters as satisfaction with the police service, crime at work, and fear of crime.

The general questions seek to establish whether anyone in the household has been a victim of any of a list of crimes—described in everyday language—in the previous year. The early 'sweeps', as they are called, realised everybody's worst fears. In 1994, for instance, there were an estimated 19 million crimes against people and their property. That seemed to be as much as four times more crime than the official statistics suggested (the difference is now somewhat lower than that). There is a trap here though, because that is only an average figure; there is a wide variation in different offences, for example almost all cases of theft of a motor vehicle are reported because of the insurance implications, but only a quarter or so of cases of vandalism. The conclusion from the BCS was that '. . . the bad news is there is a lot more crime than we thought, the good news is that most of it is petty' (Maguire, 1994).

It was also suggested (and perhaps the Home Office had an interest in making the best of a pretty bad job) that the 'statistically average person' could, among other things, 'expect' to be the victim of an assault resulting in an injury, however slight, once every century. It was also pointed out that the risk of a burglary in someone's house is less than the risk of a fire. A great deal of fear of crime was described as 'irrational', because women and the elderly, who were at the least risk of being attacked, were the groups who experienced the greatest fears.

Because there is such a 'crime differential' in different areas of residence, some criminologists, especially among the left realists, were unhappy with these comforting figures—which, they considered, distorted the 'lived realities' of women, the poor and ethnic minorities, particularly in inner city areas. A number of local crime surveys were carried out in places like Merseyside, Hammersmith, and Islington, to which I will return later. These surveys showed that there were areas where the crime situation was, indeed, much worse than the 'national average'.

FEAR OF CRIME

Victim surveys have opened up a whole new line of enquiry which has led to the fear of crime debate. This has now become a distinct social concern such that the view has been expressed that fear of crime is more of a problem than crime itself. Generally, fear of crime is taken to mean a threat to personal safety rather than a threat to property. So that meaningful research can be carried out, there are some real problems to be overcome, not all capable of easy solution, for example it is generally agreed that men are *less* likely to admit to fear but how do we know this if they are really that fearful? Then there is the problem of operationalising fear. By this sociologists mean that we must define 'fear' and then find an indicator which distinguishes 'fear' so that we recognise it when we come across it. It is not easy to phrase questions so as to measure fear. Usually fear is correlated with risk and danger. But levels of fear are far from closely related to risk. Young men—who spend a lot of time outside the home and engaging in leisure pursuits including drinking alcohol—are most at risk but admit to little fear. The elderly who leave home much less are often profoundly fearful but at little risk. Douglas (1992) points out that though we usually think of risk in terms of risk avoidance—if we are normal rational humans that is—there is also risk seeking behaviour. Walklate cites as an example the young policemen engaged in a high speed chase of other young men who are coupled in a shared desire for excitement, fear, pleasure and risk. Women are often seen as being outside this risk and risk seeking formula, but Walklate suggests that one area of risk seeking behaviour is sex where excitement and danger is to be found and there may be others. Fear, she believes, is a 'gendered phenomenon'. Betsy Stanko considers that conceptual thinking in the area of fear of crime is:

> . . . rooted in a male defined rationally based risk management view of fear which cannot tap the kinds of experiences that underpin women's responses to this issue. (Stanko, 1988)

She has coined the phrase 'climates of un-safety' to describe how women live to render themselves more or less safe in the workplace, in the home, in the street. There is more of the emotional than the rational in this, she suggests. When we turn to the actual questions used to indicate levels of fear there are more problems. 'How safe do you feel in your neighbourhood?' Here, levels of expressed safety are used as indicators of fear but is this valid? 'How much do you worry about being assaulted? Walklate says that if you ask this of an elderly person and they compare it with their worries about money and health then crime becomes relatively insignificant.

Farrel *et al* (1998) suggest that the fear of crime has been significantly misrepresented; our understanding is a product of the way that it has been recorded. Their suggestion is that quantitative methods based on surveys give a greater incidence of fear than qualitative methods based on interviews. They end to the effect that '. . . the remarkably rapid ascent of the fear of crime in a very short time in the 1980s might well in future be surpassed only by its swift demise'.

With all these difficulties in mind it can still be noted that in the second *Islington Crime Survey* of 1989 specific questions were asked about safety in the streets, on public transport and in the home. Half the women questioned felt unsafe in the home, 43 per cent felt 'a lot' or 'quite a bit' afraid on public transport and avoided it at night and there was a virtual curfew in the streets at night with nearly half of the women questioned staying in after dark.

NEW VICTIMOLOGY

We now turn to consider the Victim Movement, the 'new victimology' as it has been called.

In the 1960s and 1970s a victim movement emerged in the USA. It was rights based and in some states associated with support for the death penalty. By contrast, in the UK the victim movement emerged as Victim Support which began life as a local initiative in Bristol, in 1974. It has grown dramatically but remains without any political agenda and volunteer based. Its primary objective is to act as a good neighbour to victims of crime.

Within the criminal justice process itself we now have a *Victims Charter* which lays down how victims are to be treated, and how they are to be kept informed about the progress of their case, trial dates, and bail and sentencing decisions. In some European countries victims have considerable rights to participate in the prosecution of offenders. In Britain the victim is still essentially a witness with the difficulties that that entails. Witnesses cannot refuse to give evidence, whereas the accused is not obliged do so (although appropriate inferences may now be drawn from this by a court). Whatever the improvements that have been made to ensure that courts are user friendly, they are still an ordeal for the victim. He or she has to live again through the ordeal, in the witness box, and the rules of evidence are not always helpful: a victim may be doing the best he or she can to explain matters only to be interrupted by assertions such as 'I'm sorry you can't actually tell us that'.

The suggestion is sometimes made that victims should have a role in *sentencing* and clearly this would have psychological advantages, though whether it would outweigh any (natural) lack of objectivity is a mute point. In some states of America 'impact statements' from victims are provided to the court and taken into consideration before compensation is awarded or sentence passed and this approach has spread to areas of England and Wales (all Probation Service pre-sentence reports should now deal with the effect on the victim). The rules on compensation in magistrates' courts now favour the victim in that the maximum amount was increased to £5,000 and a compensation order takes priority over fines etc. out of the defendant's financial resources. However, it is often the case that the money is paid in very small amounts (if at all) and the periodic payment is a constant reminder to the victim of what might have been a very upsetting experience. Many people consider that the state should pay the compensation in the first place and then recover it from the guilty party. Victims may also be compensated via the Criminal Injuries Compensation Authority in cases of violence and in some other situations. Claims are evaluated on specific criteria which effectively mean that the victim must come with 'clean hands' and his or her own character and conduct is taken into account. Cynics have suggested that compensation is paid partly in recognition of the state's reliance on the victim's co-operation in bringing offenders to justice.

RESTORATIVE JUSTICE

Braithwaite's work (1989) on reintegrative shaming has provided a chance for him and others to develop a movement towards 'restorative' or 'relational justice' which is based on the philosophy that crime involves a breakdown of relationships—individual, social or communal, and that the aim should be to restore that relationship; hence, 'restorative justice', or as it is also called, redress.

Hudson (1995) writes that:

> Basic to the idea of redress are the assumptions that
> 1) what we presently call a crime is a complex event, which will have different meaning according to the circumstances of the offender, the victim and the community, and the relationships between them;
> 2) that all the parties to the event deserve a hearing, and that all have claims to the justice process.

So, restorative justice involves a non-judicial settlement of disputes through mediation or reparation in which offenders, victims and communities have their say in an atmosphere of informalism.

Perhaps the example which has sparked most interest has been 'family group conferencing', originally practised among Maoris but now used in New Zealand to deal with middle level juvenile offending.

The concept may well have an instinctive humanitarian appeal but where do we look to discover a theoretical basis for these initiatives which Bottoms has described as being rather marginal to mainstream criminal justice but which '. . . should not be dismissed given a more favourable political development' (Brownlee, 1998).

In 1990 Braithwaite and Petit produced a theory of 'republican' criminal justice. For them free citizenship in a free society which they called 'dominion' was an ideal. They argued that punishment could only be justified if it promotes desired consequences: for them an increase in overall dominion. Rather like the utilitarians in a different context (see *Chapter 2*) they sought a balance between reduction in dominion for an offender and increase in dominion for another individual. Dominion they argued must allow for an equilibrium which safeguards the interests of both victim and offender. They also embrace the notion of parsimony—in fact, they call it the 'master principle'. Parsimony, in this context, means that state-inflicted punishment should be kept to a minimum, in contrast to the desert principle. They go on to suggest that if punishment does not prevent crime then it should not be inflicted and that the ideal is a non-punitive response to crime—and so we arrive at 'restorative justice'. As an example, a victim who suffers from criminal damage would benefit more from compensation which gives him or her an opportunity to replace the property (either from money provided by the offender or the state) than if the offender is fined. If someone suffers an assault then the effect of that assault can best be restored by mediation between victim and offender when the victim may well lose the fear of further assaults. Punishment as presently meted out may actually increase that fear.

As has been implied, restorative justice involves a decision-making neighbourhood tribunal in which all parties speak for themselves, the restoration of relationships is more important than rules of procedure and at the end all parties will feel satisfied with the outcome and, above all, the undesirable event will not be repeated.

There are, not suprisingly, writers who see some problems with the method. Hudson (1998) points to two. She believes that the assumption that an agreement will be arrived at is far too readily made. In addition, she considers that there will always be some crimes so heinous that they will have to be dealt with by the criminal law. This fragmentation may lead victims dealt with by the proposed restorative justice procedures to feel that they are second class victims whose cases are not important enough for the 'real' courts.

Shapland (1988) speculates on the resistance likely to be an obstacle to this sort of reform from prison officers, judges and magistrates. She considers that this largely decentralised collection of autonomous agencies (which she compares to 'fiefdoms'), would each jealously guard their own workload and independence. In a lecture delivered in 1998 she said,

> adopting the idea of reparation or relational justice means relating it to all the rest of what police, prosecutors and courts do. Taking on board the need for a process system of justice . . . means not bolting on conferencing as an add-on for juveniles, but letting that broader value system permeate all the courts do.

The value system to which she refers includes courts becoming closer to the communities they serve 'rather than sit back, seeing their own role as rather isolated decision-makers'. She also considers that we have created a system of justice which appears to see only the decision-makers and the person who is charged with the offence—the defendant.

• • •

Chapter 8: Victimology etc. and a Look at Some Statistics—Key Points

- Von Hentig took a more interactionist stance than previous writers who had been offender oriented and suggested that some people are victim prone.
- Mendelsohn produced a typology of victims from completely innocent to most guilty.
- Wolfgang found a quarter of homicides were initiated by the victim and that nearly one fifth of rapes were victim precipitated but his definition was heavily criticised.
- There has been concern expressed at the way in which victim *proneness* becomes victim *precipitation* and then victim *blaming*.
- Mien concludes that some victims bear some responsibility for some crimes.
- Walklate is concerned that just as criminals may be perceived as falling short of 'normality' so might victims be.
- Official statistics are collected by the police who are not an agency designed for that purpose.
- The way in which an act comes to be recorded as a crime is complex and subject to attrition.

- There has long been concern about the 'dark figure', the difference between the number of crimes committed and those reported.
- *British Crime Surveys* are carried out by face-to-face interviews and in 1994 revealed 19 million crimes, about four times as much as the official statistics showed.
- Because of the difference in the amount of crime in different areas Local Crime Surveys have been carried out.
- It is considered that the fear of crime (threats to personal safety) is a distinct social problem.
- There is difficulty in defining fear so that it may be recognised: it is usually correlated with risk and danger but those least at risk (the elderly) may be the most fearful—but compared to fear about money and health, crime may become less important.
- Farrel and others have suggested that fear of crime has been misrepresented and exaggerated because of the way that it has been measured.
- There is now a *Victims' Charter* dealing with how victims are to be treated.
- It has been suggested that victims should have a role in sentencing.
- In the magistrates' court, compensation to victims takes priority but when paid in small amounts is a constant reminder to the victim.
- Victims may also be compensated by the Criminal Injuries Compensation Authority, but victims must come with 'clean hands'.
- There has been a movement towards 'restorative' or 'relational justice' where the aim is to restore the breach of the relationship broken by the crime. This involves an informal non-judicial settlement of disputes.
- Braithwaite and Petit suggest in their theory of republican criminal justice that punishment can only be justified if it increases overall dominion (free citizenship in a free society).
- They also consider parsimony (minimum of state inflicted punishment)—the 'master principle'.
- Hudson sees problems with the notion of a neighbourhood tribunal involving all parties: agreement may not be reached and there is a risk of fragmentation when some crimes still have to be dealt with by the ordinary criminal processes.
- Shapland wants the broader value system that restorative justice represents to permeate all that the courts do—and they should become closer to the communities they serve.

CHAPTER 9

Criminology: Aspects of Criminal Justice

In this final chapter, I have selected a range of quite different aspects of criminal justice with which to indicate how the thinking of criminology relates to and impacts on the system of justice *de facto* and upon day-to-day practice. These selected 'aspects' are:

- Criminal Justice Models
- Police, Policing and Law and Order
- Public Disorder
- Bail or Custody?
- Punishment and Sentencing
- Prisons
- Crime Prevention and Community Safety
- White Collar Crime.

These items could be replicated many times over in relation to other equally significant components of criminal justice. The main point is that criminology and its lessons touch upon everyday practicalities. Frequently, over time, it serves to alter the way decisions are made, the way people behave and the attitudes of people who work within, or close to, the system: for example 'victimology' (*Chapter 8*) led to the *Victims' Charter* and witness care designed to ensure proper respect for and treatment of victims of crime (not formally part of the criminal process in the UK) and people who give evidence in criminal trials. Similarly, our understanding of public disorder is informed by riots studies of flashpoints (see later in this chapter) and an awareness that their roots may lie in longstanding sociological causes inflamed by insensitive responses. Community safety has progressed from theory to statutory duty with the Crime and Disorder Act 1998.

CRIMINAL JUSTICE MODELS

Many readers of this book may be accustomed to referring to the criminal justice *system* and will have in mind a range of people who are regularly involved in it (often called 'agents') and organizations ('agencies') including police, prosecutors, the judiciary (i.e. judges and magistrates) and probation service—as well as those people in the penal system. Nicola Lacey (1994) takes a broader view and includes 'ordinary citizens' in their role as electors, reporters of incidents, witnesses, jurors, victims, offenders and lay volunteers. She also makes special mention of two further groups: politicians and the media whose role in projecting images of crime (often incorrectly) should not be overlooked.

System or process?

There has been a longstanding debate about whether we should be talking about a *system* or a *process*—whoever or whatever we choose to include in it—or, indeed, about what I have heard one academic use, though I think unfairly, a criminal justice *lottery*.

It is a system in the sense that all its parts are interdependent and that a change in one part will have repercussions elsewhere. If the local police need to handle a number of serious crimes simultaneously there are likely to be less charges of a more minor nature, less work for the Crown Prosecution Service, less for the local bench and so on. Many commentators deny that this interdependence is sufficient to make it a system and that what we really have is a number of independent functions with the court often placed at the centre. Cavadino and Dignan (1992) refer to the arrangements as 'dysfunctional', because the different parts have different objectives which are sometimes competing. In his report, after the 1990 prison riots, Lord Woolf proposed closer co-operation between different parts of the system and, as a result, the Criminal Justice Consultative Council with its area committees was established as a focal point for representatives of the various agencies.

What are 'models of criminal justice'?

To assist in an understanding of the way that any system operates and of its function it is helpful to have models—though readers will not actually find the particular models I am about to describe anywhere in pure form. They are simply useful explanatory tools and produce valuable insights into the way courts and other parts of the system work. Herbert Packer (1968) identified two models:

- **The 'crime control' model**
  The function of the crime control model (sometimes compared to an assembly line) is *punishment*. There is a presumption that, if the case has reached court, then the defendant is guilty—otherwise the police and the prosecutor would have filtered the case out. The crime control model is thus supportive of the police, and conviction rates are high. Other features include: the notion that people are assumed to be responsible for their actions; that the priority is the conviction of the guilty; and that if an innocent person is punished in error (the model allows for the possibility of mistakes) this is the price of controlling crime.

- **The due process model**
  The function of the due process model (sometimes compared to an obstacle course in contrast to an assembly line) is to deliver *justice*. The court is a neutral referee between the individual and the state. There is a real presumption of innocence and the defendant enjoys many legal safeguards. The priority is the acquittal of the innocent. Other features of the model are: that it stresses the possibility of error in fact finding so that there is a need for further review of decisions (an appeals system); the doctrine of legal guilt in contrast to factual guilt (technicalities and procedures are deemed important in achieving of justice); and the high test whereby criminal allegations must be proved 'beyond reasonable doubt'.

  At this point we should note the views of Doreen McBarnet (1981). She asked why, when the rhetoric of justice is all about it being better that ten guilty men go free than one innocent man is wrongly convicted, the vast majority of accused people are found guilty. She contends that the ideology of the law is 'due process' but that the substantive law works for 'crime control'. For example, the ideology of the law is strong on the rights of suspects but this is not carried over into statute because of the width of police discretion. The problem, she says, is not police misconduct but the laxity of the law itself. On that basis Packer's distinction is a false one.

  Other writers like David Smith, notably in 'Case Construction and the Goals of Criminal Process' (*British Journal of Criminology*, 37:3) points out that crime control is of necessity the goal of criminal process and the criminal justice system cannot be understood or justified without reference to that objective. Due process values are needed because they help to achieve the goal of convicting the guilty and of protecting us from an arbitrary and whimsical system.

Michael King (1981) offered four further models of criminal justice:

- **The medical model**
  The function here is treatment and rehabilitation. The court gathers information about the defendant and expert advice is recognised, with the defendant responded to as an individual and an understanding that people are not always responsible for their actions.

- **The bureaucratic model**
  The function here is management, speed and efficiency with the most economic use of resources paramount. Procedures are

standardised and individuals processed according to these, with the minimum of friction. Time-saving methods are applauded and, for example reduced sentences given in exchange for guilty pleas.

- **The status passage model**
  The function here is denunciation and degradation with an emphasis on ritual and ceremony, with public condemnation of the defendants' behaviour. The press has a role in publicising information about individuals who have offended against the law and this is seen as maintaining the community's values. (Many commentators see elements of this model in other explanations of the system).

- **.The power model**
  The function here is the maintenance of class domination. Wherever discretion exists within the system, it is used to serve the goals of the powerful. There are gaps between the rhetoric that 'everyone is equal before the law' and the reality. The supposed existence of this model is part of the reason, I suspect, for the continuing criticism that judges and magistrates are unrepresentative and drawn largely from the middle-class. Whatever efforts have been made to correct this, Dignan and Wynne were confirming in 1997 that the magistracy did not represent a microcosm of society in 'social composition, political allegiance or social affiliations' (*British Journal of Criminology*, 37: 184-197).

Bottoms and McClean (1976) proposed what they called a 'liberal bureaucratic' model (which, incidentally, they suggested, was supported by humane and enlightened clerks to the justices). This model differed from the crime control model in that it sought justice and protected the rights of individuals, but also differed from the due process model in that it set a limit to that protection. If it did not, then the whole process might grind to a halt as defendants 'tried it on'. The twin objectives of the liberal bureaucratic model are defending the rights of individuals and administrative efficiency, with the latter of overriding importance if these objectives conflict. Andrew Rutherford (1994) makes a somewhat similar but wider point when he asserts that the values and beliefs that shape the daily work and concerns of criminal justice practitioners (by which he means police, probation officers, CPS, court officials, judges, magistrates and prison staff) fall into three 'working credos'.

1. The punishment credo: the aim of which is the punitive degradation of offenders.

2. The efficiency credo: which is about management, pragmatism, and expediency.
3. The caring credo: liberal and humanitarian values.

He goes on to point out that '. . . human values have a precarious existence in the criminal justice process'.

McConville *et al* (1991) suggest that the crime control and the due process models exist simultaneously and uneasily, and certainly Packer never intended that they should be seen as exclusionary, as direct alternatives. Similarly, their relative importance varies over time. The authors go on to say that in the 1970s and 1980s due process was predominant with many people (particularly the police) feeling that the pendulum had swung too much in favour of the defendant. While Michael Howard was home secretary (1994 to 1997) the swing was towards crime control, and it is not discernible that this has yet started to move back again with the 'New Labour' government.

In their controversial *The Case for the Prosecution* (1991), McConville *et al* deal with what they call 'case construction'. Their work was the result of a two year study of police and prosecutorial decision-making which demonstrated that the police had a great deal of power in the prosecution process and that this had not been restrained by the Police and Criminal Evidence Act 1984 (which among other things introduced the PACE Codes for the treatment of suspects). In essence the authors claim that the police dominate every aspect of the criminal process, from the identification of suspects and their investigation and arrest to decisions concerning detention, charge and the collection of evidence. In this sense, the Crown Prosecution Service (which should review the evidence and police decisions to bring accusations) is subservient to the police because the contents of the file that the prosecutor receives contains what the police want it to contain—and it is often not examined over-critically because the vast majority of defendants plead guilty, whether the case against them is strong or weak. Thus the file is presented in a 'uni-directional way' and accepted by the prosecutor. They go on to suggest that the law-enforcers (the police) play a leading role in deciding who the criminals are. It is the police who construct the population of suspects, mainly young, male, working class and disproportionately black.

The evidence that is presented as 'independent' or 'credible' may itself be the product of decisions made by the police (*British Journal of Criminology*, 37:3). McConville *et al* suggest that the only way to deal with this is to overturn the whole of police culture, a subject that we will return to when we examine *Police and Law and Order* (next section).

Criminal Justice Models—Key Points

- There is a debate about whether we should refer to a *system* (all the parts being 'interdependent') or a *process* (partly because of the dysfunctional nature of the parts with their individual objectives).
- Packer identified two models: crime control and due process.
- King added four other models: medical, bureaucratic, status passage, power.
- Bottoms and McClean added the liberal bureaucratic model with the twin objectives of defending the rights of individuals and administrative efficiency—the latter of overriding importance.
- McBarnet argues that although the ideology of the law may be due process the substantive law works for crime control.
- The authors of *The Case for the Prosecution* refer to 'case construction' and claim that the file as presented to the CPS is 'uni-directional' and evidence the product of decisions made by the police.

• • •

POLICE, POLICING AND LAW AND ORDER

Wherever the law draws a line, the police are requested to hold it . . . As a society we lay upon them the responsibility for discharging what may be mutually irreconcilable responsibilities: they must enforce the law impartially, defend the liberties of the citizen, while maintaining public order and the Queen's Peace.

Stuart Hall (1980)

Firstly, we must draw an important distinction implied in the title of this section: police and policing are not synonymous. *Police* refers to a particular institution not found in every society particularly those of a pre-industrial type. As Robert Reiner (1984) writes:

The police are mainly a body of people patrolling public places in blue uniforms, with a broad mandate of crime control, order maintenance and some negotiable social service function.

As this 'broad mandate' suggests and, as we all know, the police are called upon to perform a bewildering variety of tasks from traffic control to combating armed terrorists. As Bittner (1974) points out, the uniting feature of these tasks involves 'something that ought not to be happening and about which someone had better do something *now*'. P A J Waddington calls the police the social equivalent of the Automobile

Association or Royal Automobile Club who provide a provisional solution but who are neither car makers nor road builders. What distinguishes the police from other citizens is that deposited with them is the state's monopoly of legitimate power within its territory. 'The men who walk our streets as community bobbies today are equipped and ready to take them by force tomorrow' (Northam, 1988).

Policing is a much wider concept and, rather than being an institution, is a process. It seems likely that no social order could exist without it. It can be carried out by a wide variety of people of which *the police* are but one aspect, and a variety of methods. It includes what is sometimes called 'hybrid policing', for example municipal police, and also professionals engaged by security firms, the public, employees of firms whether engaged for that specific purpose or simply 'keeping their eyes open', and all the modern technology of 'policing' of which the security camera is the most obvious example. Such has been the extent of the privatisation of policing (the total number of security guards is well in excess of the number of operational police officers) that some writers question whether the state is any longer the embodiment of public authority.

It is only in comparatively recent times that criminologists and sociologists have turned their attention from criminals to the police. The seminal British work was Bainton's, *The Policeman in the Community*. This was published in 1964 at a time when the public's questioning of the police was growing. It involved observing and interviewing officers and was trend-setting.

One of the things that writers found, when researching the police, which seems to have caused some surprise was the phenomenon of 'police discretion', i.e. that the police do not always enforce the law and clear evidence of a violation of the law does not always result in criminal proceedings. If it was otherwise, of course, the sheer volume would overwhelm the system. 'Police officers necessarily use their personal judgement to weigh up a situation and enforce the law' (Scraton, 1985). In fact, going a step further, Lord Scarman in his 1981 report, took the view that when there was a conflict, public tranquillity had priority over law enforcement. Once it is accepted as an inevitable feature of police work that there are occasions when the law is under-enforced the question then arises whether all sections of the community benefit equally from this. In 1990, Morgan *et al* in a study of people in custody in police stations found that the overwhelming majority of those people detained were from that group referred to as the 'police property' element of the economically and socially marginalised. Lee (1981) explains that 'a category becomes police property when the dominant powers of society . . . leave the problems of the social control of that category to the police'. The data from Morgan's study suggests that police discretion is not exercised in favour of young, unemployed males and there are numerous studies suggesting that it is exercised disproportionately against black people. It has been pointed out that police resources are largely devoted to patrolling public spaces and the lower the class of a particular person the more of his or her social life tends to take place outside the home and thus he or she is more likely to come to the attention of the police. People are not usually arrested for activities carried out in the living room, but what if the 'living room' is in the street?

It appears that the police do routinely, in practice, depart from the Rule of Law (which asserts that 'all are equal') and the question is then how are they able to do it. The answer lies in the low visibility of much police work. As James Q Wilson (1975) puts it, 'Discretion increases as one moves down the hierarchy'. Where policy really counts is in the streets. The former Policy Studies Institute (1983) drew a distinction between three sets of rules when exploring the differences between legal rules and police practice:

- *working rules:* which underpin police practice and which are derived from the culture of the police and whose relationship with official rules and policy are problematic
- *inhibitory rules:* which are the official rules and likely to be enforced, so that they are taken into account even if disagreeable; and
- *presentation rules:* which are used to import the proper subsequent gloss to actions carried out under the 'working rules'.

(Similar rules are probably to be found in many workplaces in some form or other).

The Police and Criminal Evidence Act 1984 (PACE) was largely aimed at reducing deviation from the Rule of Law, but Reiner is not alone in suggesting that changes in culture cannot be brought about by changes in the formal rules alone. As a custody sergeant told Dixon *et al* (1989):

> . . . the bobby out on the street . . . He's got to make an instant decision; sometimes the rules and regulations go by the board and he uses his common sense. Then he may find when he comes into the police station that . . . he's used a power that he didn't have. Then we have to find him a power.

In connection with some of the shortcomings of PACE, Wasik *et al* (1999) refer to section 37 which requires a custody officer to scrutinise the reasons for detaining a suspect as soon as he or she is brought into a police station. This, the authors say, has had almost no effect in practice:

'It is exceptional for a custody officer to disallow the detention of a suspect'. Likewise, section 58 refers to the requirement to give a suspect information about the right to legal advice but Sanders and Bridges reported in 1990 that in 12 per cent of cases the police failed to inform suspects of their right, misrecorded a request or used 'ploys' to avoid summoning an adviser or delayed doing so until the request was dropped or forgotten. A revision of the Code of Practice in 1991 improved matters but in 1992 Brown *et al* found that 26 per cent of suspects were being informed 'unclearly'. Finally, Moston and Stephenson (1993) found that eight per cent of suspects were interviewed prior to arrival at the police station which is in direct contravention of the PACE Codes of Practice.

Clearly police discretion is very important to an understanding of police work and it is necessary to try and find an explanation as to the reason or reasons for it operating as it does. There are two main approaches to this: through the individual and through 'cop culture'. There is also the question of how discretion is controlled.

Individualistic explanations

Is a particular sort of individual drawn to police work, to whom 'helmet and truncheon' have a particular appeal? It has been suggested that police recruits have more authoritarian or prejudiced personalities than normal and some research supports that view (particularly that of Coleman and Gorman in 1982: but this has been criticised by Butler (1982) on methodological grounds). On the other hand, it seems just as likely that such an outlook may result from the socialisation process *after* recruitment.

Cultural explanations

It is said that three characteristics of police work lead to a particular culture. These are:

- *Danger* Although there are other dangerous occupations it is the unpredictable risk that characterises police work: the routine tap on a door may lead to confrontation with an armed person.
- *Authority* This is interdependent with danger. It is the other side of the coin: having the authority that brings the danger.
- *Constant pressure* Which is to be *efficient* rather than *legal*: the officer who cannot produce results is 'no good'.

This is nicely illustrated by an ex-detective sergeant who told of a notice pinned up in a CID office: 'A sus a day keeps the helmet away' (Wasik *et al*, 1999).

The most common explanation for the attitude and behaviour of police officers is found in what is sometimes called 'canteen culture'. In an article full of insights in the Spring 1999 edition of the *British Journal of Criminology*, P A J Waddington argues that the canteen culture is more about what police officers say than what they do and that some writers at least find the police culture convenient as a tool of condemnation for injustices in the criminal justice system. Waddington believes that '. . . the canteen culture is a "repair shop" of policing and jokes, banter and anecdote the tools'.

In 1966, Skolnick's pioneering study of detectives in California gave rise to what he called the policeman's 'working personality' which is much the same. The characteristics of the culture that Skolnick singled out have been expanded upon by other commentators.

Suspiciousness
Most police officers are 'never off duty' and will tell of matchboxes and odd bits of paper covered in car numbers. A problem is that stereotyping is a tool of suspicion. The reason why the officer looks at a person with suspicion is often because he is the sort of person that he knows he ought to look at with suspicion because he complies with some stereotype or other. It has been suggested that this stereotyping of likely offenders may become a self-fulfilling prophecy leading to the sort of deviance amplification discussed in earlier chapters.

Internal solidarity and social isolation
Many police officers find it easier to mix socially with other officers. This may be for simple reasons like the odd hours of work but it is also much easier to relax away from the hostility or fear which members of the public often display towards the police. There is a 'them and us' attitude not only between those 'in the job' and those not, but also between the 'street cops' and the 'management cops' (who are derided by the former). As far as internal solidarity is concerned there is an expectation that one will not be let down by colleagues and will be backed up by others, whether it is during an incident on the street or in a disciplinary matter.

Mission
Police work is not just a job but a way of life, almost a religion. It is fun, it is exciting, chasing villains is the best of all games. The policeman is indispensable and without the 'thin blue line' there would be anarchy.

Machismo
This is still largely a man's world. There is often a great deal of drinking as part of the job and, because of the glamour, 'there is always a bit of

spare round the corner'. Reiner (1992) writes: 'One hazard of police research is the taking of mental notes while sinking under a bar as the consumption of pints mounts'.

Conservatism
It has been said in the past that policeman tend to be conservative both politically and morally. Because the organization is tightly disciplined, officers with a conservative outlook fit in better. Reiner reports on a narrow conventional morality although as indicated above, the culture could not be described as puritan. It is a response to the three characteristics of the job mentioned above and any changes in police attitudes and behaviour that society might want to bring about must have regard to that. Of course, policemen are not all the same. Researchers have identified four basic variants:

- the *peace keepers* are the bobbies who are more interested in maintaining public tranquillity on the patch than pursuing villains, they are fulfilled by being patrol officers
- the *law enforcers* believe that real policing is about catching criminals, that they should be left to get on with it, without interference from above and without too many rules that are seen as assisting the criminals and hampering them
- the *alienated cynics* or *uniform carriers* are merely serving time. Disillusioned by failure they are doing as little work as possible
- the *professionals* are ambitious for promotion and refrain from canteen chatter about 'the bosses'. If they fail to become management cops they are likely to end up as uniform carriers.

That there are also cultural variation between forces was noted by James Q Wilson in *Varieties of Police Behaviour* (1968). Wilson drew a distinction between:

- *watchman style:* where the emphasis is on order maintenance rather than law enforcement, and where officers have a wide discretion
- *legalistic style:* where by contrast there is a minimum of discretion and law enforcement is all important; and
- *service style:* which sets out to be helpful to the citizen with formal cautioning rather than charging.

These examples are from America where the situation is somewhat different but in England in 1983 Jones and Levi examined public attitudes in two forces which could hardly have provided more of a contrast: Devon and Cornwall where the chief constable was John Alderson, the father of community policing, and Manchester where

James Anderton took a tough law and order approach. They found that the public in Devon and Cornwall had more favourable judgements of their police than those in Manchester and also that the Devon and Cornwall police had a more accurate perception of their standing with the public. It would be easy to conclude that these results had more to do with rural and city contexts than policing style but the contrast still held good when the researchers also compared Plymouth and Wigan. It is also interesting that cop culture seems to survive in the most extreme situations as in Northern Ireland's in the recent past. Quoting a member of the RUC, Magee (1991) writes: 'Riots? Well, put it like this, most of the boys enjoy them. There's not a bit of fear. It's a big game really'.

In the latest of his own works, *Principled Policing,* Alderson (1998) argues that policing can be viewed as based on the social contract as advanced by Rawls, which is essentially 'justice as fairness'. Dealing with situations as diverse as the policing of Northern Ireland, China's Tianenman Square (where state police shot dead huge numbers of demonstrators), Nazi Germany and the British miners strike of 1984/5, he demonstrates the need for policing to remain independent of government and argues that, unless supplied by police commanders (what Alderson calls 'high police'), policing lacks any fundamental values of morality, decency or fairness. He also demonstrates how, through factors of the kind outlined earlier in this chapter, standards of police behaviour can rapidly deteriorate.

The control of police discretion
The English common law has developed a somewhat controversial doctrine of 'constabulary independence'. Lord Denning said of a chief police officer: 'He is answerable to the law alone, and a chief inspector of constabulary . . . a chief constable is answerable to God, his Queen and his conscience'. We must assume that this doctrine is applicable to all constables, since in theory there is no difference between them.

There are, of course, mechanisms for holding officers accountable for individual decisions and senior officers accountable for force policy. Individuals may have an action taken against them in the civil courts for wrongful use of their powers and there is a complaints procedure which members of the public can use. The Police Act 1976 set up the Police Complaints Board, whose powers were limited to reviewing the papers assembled by police investigators. The Police Complaints Authority set up under the Police and Criminal Evidence Act 1984 had more investigative powers, but did not satisfy those who called for independent investigations. The present system seems to have failed to command confidence among complainants and the public. Although the idea of independence sounds right, another view is put by one of the chief constables interviewed by Reiner who said:

Independent investigation sounds very attractive but I think it will create more problems than it would solve . . . You've got to run right quickly before anybody has an opportunity to destroy the traces . . . they couldn't pull the wool over my eyes. The bad guys will get away with it far easier than they appear to be doing at the moment if it was an independent investigation.

Accountability for force policy comes, in theory, through a tripartite structure:

- *chief constables:* who have 'direction and control' of the force
- *local police authorities*: who are charged with the 'maintenance of an efficient and effective police force'; and
- *the home secretary*: with an overview of the efficiency of police forces throughout the country (and direct responsibilities with regard to the Metropolitan police in London).

However, the prevalent academic view is that the structure is heavily skewed and the Home Office has become by far the most powerful part of that structure. This became clear in 1988 when Northumbria Police Authority sought judicial review of a Home Office circular which offered to supply CS gas or plastic bullets from a central store to any chief constable not permitted by his authority to purchase them. The Court of Appeal decided that the home secretary was not acting beyond his powers because he had a power under the Royal Prerogative. In the same year, Uglow (1988) reports that at the time of the miners strike the home secretary had a meeting with chief constables and instructed them not to allow financial constraints to interfere with the operational discharge of their duties: this action was taken without the knowledge of the local police authorities. Reiner refers to the 'fig leaf' of local influence in a highly centralised, *de facto* national structure.

The police: Where now?
That the police have undergone a major change in the last 25 years is hardly deniable. This is particularly noticeable in the field of public order. We have seen the change from the time when 'the police who held back a demonstrating crowd or picketing workers were not some alien force, but the ordinary coppers who told people the time, returned lost children to their parents and prevented crime' (Waddington, 1991) to them being, 'unrecognisable in visors, NATO style crash helmets and fireproof overalls advancing behind transparent shields' (Jefferson, 1990). Some writers, like Tim Newburn found the defining moment the 'Battle of Orgreave' during the miners' strike of 1984/1985 when horses were used to charge the crowd and 'snatch squads' used to make arrests.

Waddington described the scene as a 'medieval battle ground'. There is an ongoing debate whether this drift into para-militarism is the result of a growing level of violence to which the police, to their regret have had to respond (Waddington), or whether it has been because of a crisis of authority resulting from a breakdown of consensus and involving some sort of conspiracy between the police, the judiciary and the government (Jefferson).

Certainly the police have been involved in a number of scandals involving both corruption and miscarriages of justice, have been accused of racial discrimination and, indeed, institutionalised racism and have appeared to be unable to stem rising crime. The truth about this last matter is surely that 'Crime is the product of deeper social forces largely beyond the ambit of any policing tactics' (Reiner, 1994). Reiner's grim warning for the future is that '. . . for those who can afford it the provision of security will be increasingly privatised' and '. . . the police will be replaced by an assortment of bodies with policing functions. Police officers can no longer be totems symbolising a cohesive social order which no longer exists'.

Police, Policing and Law and Order—Key Points

- The police are an institution: a body of people with a broad mandate and the state's monopoly of legitimate power
- Policing is a process of social control of which the police are one part.
- Police discretion which arises from the low visibility of much police work means that the law is not always enforced.
- The question whether all sections of the community benefit equally from police discretion is usually answered in the negative.
- PACE was aimed at reducing departures from the rule of law.
- Characteristics of police work are: danger, authority and pressure: this leads to a 'police culture' typified by suspiciousness, solidarity and isolation, mission, machismo and conservatism.
- Different types of policemen exist: peace keepers, law enforcers, uniform carriers, professionals.
- Different types of force exist: watchman, legalistic, service.
- Police discretion is controlled individually either thorough the courts or the complaints.
- Force accountability is through: chief constables, local police authorities, the home secretary—but a strong academic view is that the Home Office is the most powerful part of this tripartite structure.

• • •

PUBLIC DISORDER

> To merely dismiss the rioting as "mindless hooliganism and yobbery" is to remain blind to the true reasons for its occurrence and to guarantee that it will return with shocking devastation to punish us for our indifference and complacency.
>
> David Waddington, 1992

There is nothing new about public disorder and collective violence in this 'green and pleasant land'. Those who described the violence in the 1980s as 'alien to our streets' were suffering from 'historical amnesia'.

Eric Hobsbawm, the social historian wrote: 'No other European country has as strong a tradition of rioting as Britain'. A few examples will make the point: the Peasants' Revolt of 1381, the Gordon Riots 1780, the Sunday Trading Riots 1855, 'Bloody Sunday' 1887, Liverpool police strike 1919, the Hunger marches and the Fascist marches in the 1930s and the Peace campaign violence of the 1960s. To this sorry litany can now be added—and these are but a few examples—Brixton, Handsworth, Blackbird Leys (Oxford), Ely Estates (Cardiff), Meadow Well (Newcastle), Broadwater Farm, Toxteth and St. Giles (Lincoln).

In this section I will examine some of the explanations given for rioting and look at some of the causal factors. The first theory, if such it can be called, is the conspiracy theory—of which Martin Kettle in *The Guardian* of 2 April 1990 wrote 'There has never been a riot in British history where someone hasn't claimed that the whole thing was a conspiracy by a minority'. Another explanation is the 'riff-raff' theory; rioters are the criminals, the deviants and the rootless, the 'rent-a-mob'. One of the rioters who took part in the anti-poll tax march in London wrote afterwards: 'But the crowd . . . was overwhelmingly a *normal-looking* bunch of people . . .' Again, as Kettle says, 'Rioting may be wrong but it deserves to be analysed seriously'.

At least two further theories have their roots in a work entitled *The Crowd* dating from the last century by Le Bon (1895) in which he wrote,

> By the mere fact that he forms part of a crowd a man descends several rungs in the ladder of civilisation . . . He possesses the spontaneity, the violence, the ferocity . . . of primitive beings.

From this has come the social facilitation approach of Allport (1924): there is a sort of circular chain reaction in which each individual becomes trapped in a spiral of rising excitement and emotion. Zimbardo (1969) suggests that individuals become anonymous and lose their self-awareness and so are able to act without restraint. Gaskell and Benewick (1987) express clearly the objection to this approach:

Such individualistic theories appear to explain the homogeneity of the crowd but do so at the cost of predicting bedlam in every crowd, at Ascot and the Lynch mob alike.

Other theories like the frustration-aggression hypothesis which sees rioting as an emotional outburst due to frustration caused by blocked goals or hot weather (Berkowitz, 1972) or relative deprivation (Gurr, 1970), appeal to common sense but fail to answer the question: 'But why at that place at that time and not at some other place and time?'.

Two major theories remain to be examined, those of Neil Smelser (1972) and David Waddington (1992), which go some way to providing an answer. Smelser believes that rioting is irrational and deviant and the groups that engage in such activity are experiencing 'social strain', e.g. because expectations perceived as legitimate are not being met or basic rights are being ignored. The second concept that Smelser uses is 'structural conduciveness' which is characterised by:

- the presence of an agency to blame for the unsatisfactory state of affairs (usually the police)
- the failure of proper channels for airing the grievances; and
- the possibility of communication among those that are aggrieved.

Where social strain is present and conditions are structurally conducive a 'general hostile belief' may develop and then a single rumour or incident may cause an 'hostile outburst'. How far disorder then spreads depends on the social-control agencies reacting decisively. Among the critics of the theory are King and Brearly (1996) who write that '. . . it fails to take account of the essential rationality of much crowd behaviour and possible contributions of police action to the development and activity of crowds'.

The 'flash points' model of David Waddington postulates that disorder is likely to occur at a number of different levels:

- *at the structural level*: where a section of society feels that it is being deprived of something, either material or the chance to 'make it'
- *at the political level*: where the dissenting group, as we shall call them, feels alienated from political and legal systems
- *at the cultural level*: where activities that the group regards as legitimate are unacceptable to the police
- *at the contextual level*: where, perhaps, the recent history of exchanges between the police and the dissenting group have been negative, where there have been rumours of trouble, where the mass media have exacerbated a difficult situation, where police

intelligence has caused the police to prepare for the worst, where, in fact, all the ingredients of a self-fulfilling prophecy exist
- *at the situational level*: where, e.g. the group looks upon certain areas as cultural territory to be defended or are regarded by the police as areas they must patrol to prevent 'no-go' areas; and
- *at the interactional level:* where police and the dissenting group actually meet and where the 'flashpoint' may occur. Waddington describes the flash point as an action that breaks the unwritten rules governing behaviour between the parties. It may be an uncompromising police arrest or a brick thrown at the police.

Lord Scarman, describing the events in Brixton of 11 April 1981 wrote, 'The tinder for a major conflagration was there: the arrest outside the S & M Car Hire office was undoubtedly the spark that set it ablaze'. This is clearly expressed in 'flashpoint' model terms. What happened was that two plain clothes policemen stopped a mini-cab driver who they thought had pushed a small quantity of drugs down his right ankle sock (it was actually a wad of pound notes). Nevertheless, having realised this they continued to search his cab in what Robin Auld QC described as a 'needless display of authority, just another of the many examples of needless police harassment to add to many'. A crowd gathered and some uniformed officers arrived. Accusations of 'planting' were levelled at the police. A black youth was arrested and removed in a police van. An officer called for reinforcements when he believed, wrongly, that a colleague had been injured. The major conflagration that followed involved 145 buildings damaged, 207 vehicles damaged or destroyed, 450 people injured, 354 arrests. The events tied up 7,300 police officers.

Other well known flash points include: the accidental shooting of Mrs Groce; the heart attack suffered by Cynthia Jarrett when police searched her house; and the arrest of Asian youths playing football—in Brixton (1985), Broadwater Farm (1985) and Bradford (1995) respectively. The flashpoint model also goes some way to explaining why riots *do not* happen. In 1981, for example there was some civil disturbance in Sheffield but there was no flashpoint and no riot because the pre-history of the relationship between the parties was one of co-operation.

At least some of what are considered causal factors of urban riots have been implicitly referred to in the last section, *Police, Policing and Law and Order*. Lord Scarman concluded that unemployment, education, poor housing and lack of amenities were contributory factors which, with others, 'form a set of "social conditions" which create a predisposition towards violent protest'. Certainly, deprivation of all types, both absolute and relative, lies at the heart of much urban rioting. Keith (1993) in examining the Brixton riots of 1981 notes that in the Railton Road area where the S & M office was situated, only 22 of the 400 properties were, in the Council's view, in a satisfactory state of repair. Field and Southgate (1982) found that unemployment and the resulting boredom were cited as the most common reason given for the riots. In particular, unemployment among the black community is disproportionately high in urban areas and what jobs there are usually unskilled and low paid. Inner city schools tend not to attract investment or the best teachers which itself leads to poor prospects for school leavers.

I have already referred to the matter of territoriality. The 1980 riot in St Paul's, Bristol, which should have alerted the authorities to what might be to come, revolved around a cafe, described by Kettle and Hodges as the only bit of territory they (the local youth) had left, which was raided by the police. Rioters drove the police out of the St Paul's region but no further. The incident can be seen as a defence of territory. A further factor, which almost all writers refer to, is bad relationships between the police and young black people described by one writer as 'visceral hatred' of the police. Lea and Young (1984) emphasised the marginalisation of young people 'from the political process of liberal democracy'. They point out that in the past the working class incorporated itself into the political system through the trades union movement and the membership of political parties. Now a great many unemployed people have never had work. They know—and care—nothing for the traditions of social reform. Civil disorder is now perceived as the only way to bring pressure to bear on the powerful.

Copy-catting

Finally, I must note the danger of media contagion or 'copy- catting'. Hytner (1981) refers to the Moss Side rioting of 1981 being initiated by a group of white youths taunting their black friends that they were slower than their Brixton and Toxteth brethren.

Football 'hooligans'

In any discussion on public disorder space must be found for a reference, however brief, to football hooliganism. Although the 'hey-day' of this sort of behaviour was in the mid-1980s, when the problem was so bad that English teams were banned from European competition, there are still outbreaks, thankfully sporadic, but little room for complacency given events involving English supporters at the World Cup in France in 1998. However, it would be a mistake to think of this as a new phenomenon. Dunning (1984) for example refers to reports in the *Leicester Mercury* of pitch invasions and other forms of crowd disorder as early as the 1890s.

Melnick (1986) listed the main constituents of this sort of misbehaviour as: physical assaults on opposition fans and the police, verbal abuse, vandalism, drunkenness, pitch invasions, theft, and possession of offensive weapons. It is misleading to think that violence connected with football occurs most frequently *inside* the ground because, as police surveillance methods have improved, so the violence has tended to move to shopping centres, public houses, railway stations and roads around grounds where rival fans come into contact. Research has shown that those most involved are white, working-class males between 17 and 20. Far from them being only marginally interested in the game itself—and we have often heard that they are not real fans—Dunning *et al* (1986) suggested that hooligans are among the most committed and knowledgeable.

Smith (1983) draws an interesting distinction between 'issue-oriented' riots where there is some 'legitimating belief', for example bitterness stemming from a disallowed goal, a denial of access to the ground, and 'issueless riots', for example high spirits accompanying victory or 'time out' riots. With regard to the latter, Smith writes:

> Most of the scholarly literature on the subject suggests that hooligans are as much motivated by the desire for fun, excitement, and peer status as they are by ethnic, regional or other animosities.

Turning to some theoretical explanations for football hooliganism, Ian Taylor (1983) sees it as an attempt by working class fans to recover control of a game that was once peculiarly 'theirs'. Modern changes like the emphasis on comfort, with expensive executive boxes, the enormous salaries paid to players (no longer do the stars arrive at the ground on the same bus as the fans) and commercial initiatives, together with the internationalisation of the game have destroyed the illusion that the fans were part of the team's affairs. It should be noted that most English clubs started out as working class occupational groups, for example West Ham United was formed by workers at an iron works. Taylor refers to a 'subcultural rump' of the working class section of the crowd (as opposed to the new middle class element) for whom, when the fans invade the pitch when a goal is disallowed, it may be a way of hoping *magically* to reverse the referee's decision. To be arrested while fighting opposition supporters is to convey to the management the nature of the 'really genuine' supporter. More recently, Taylor (1989) has amended his view and has divided the youth population into: 'the upwardly mobile', who can afford to travel overseas where they display 'nationalistic aggression' towards foreign fans; and the less affluent underclass of young males who have no prospects of steady jobs and no well integrated community to support them with the result that hooligan activity provides them with self-esteem they badly need and once would have obtained elsewhere. This later view of Taylor's, which is reminiscent of Phil Cohen's sub-cultural theory (*Chapter 6*) is similar to

Wragg (1984) who perceives hooliganism as a way of 'trying to recover magically territory, both physical and cultural, that they have lost', through the decline of established trades, massive rehousing projects and the breakdown of whole communities and neighbourhoods. Phil Cohen and Robins (1978) in a study of Arsenal supporters emphasise this territoriality: 'It is as if, for these youngsters, the space they share on the North Bank is a way of magically retrieving the sense of group solidarity and identification that once went with living in a traditional working class neighbourhood'. The recurring references to 'magic' in this passage resonate with the views of Hall and the Birmingham School (pp.74, 107).

Peter Marsh (1978) sees football hooliganism as a ritualised expression of aggression demonstrating dominance and masculinity: the 'aggro' is rule-governed and the chants, gestures and stares are relatively harmless and seldom result in injury. Critics of this approach—apart from suggesting that it ignores the class-specific nature of football hooliganism—also point out that it seriously underestimates how severe some of the violence is.

Dunning (1990) suggests that middle class children are exposed to parents who emphasise self-control to their children: lower-working-class boys indulge in rough, masculine forms of play often without adult supervision. In the family there is more likely to be physical punishment and feuds within and between families. Toughness is to be valued and as the boys grow up it is the ability to fight, not their education and employment—for they have none—from which they derive status. This socialisation process delights under the name 'sociogenesis of masculine aggression'. Critics of this approach suggest that Dunning may have overstated the extent of lower working class involvement.

I have noted that football hooliganism dates back to the nineteenth century

> but the specific forms of hooliganism are new; football crowds were not segregated before the 1960s; youth did not congregate around football clubs as their territory—they had a larger territory and community which they shared with their older male relatives. (Holt, 1989)

Public Disorder—Key Points

- Britain has a strong tradition of rioting going back many centuries.
- Many explanations of rioting have been offered; the most widely accepted is David Waddington's 'flash points' model.
- Causal factors of urban riots include: unemployment, poor education, poor housing and lack of amenities.
- Disorder at football matches is not a new phenomenon.
- Football hooligans are often committed and knowledgeable.

- Smith draws a distinction between 'issue orientated' and 'issueless' riots.
- Theoretical explanations include: the working class trying to recover control of their game, the ritualised expression of aggression and masculinity; and the fact that in lower working class families the ability to fight may bring status

• • •

BAIL OR CUSTODY?

I cannot understand why so many people are remanded in custody. Of the people with whom I spent my five months on remand, it seemed to me that very few represented any kind of threat to society.

Audrey Peckam (1985)

Only a very few cases brought before magistrates are disposed of at the first hearing. Generally speaking, when the defendant appears on summons the magistrates have a discretion whether simply to adjourn the case to a later date or to remand him or her. When the defendant appears on a police charge, the person will either be remanded on unconditional bail (itself a misnomer because there is a condition: of reappearance at a stated date and time, otherwise an offence is committed), bail with conditions attached, or in custody.

The decision is governed by the provisions of the Bail Act 1976. Section 4 of the 1976 Act provides that a person shall be granted bail unless certain exceptions provided in Schedule 1 of the Act apply. Paragraph 2 of the Schedule provides that bail *need not* be granted if the court is satisfied that there are *substantial grounds* (this seems to mean more than just a possibility, but less than beyond a reasonable doubt) for believing that if bail was granted the defendant would:

- fail to surrender to custody
- commit an offence while on bail; and
- interfere with witnesses or otherwise obstruct the course of justice.

The grounds upon which these reasons may be based include:

- the nature and seriousness of the offence and the probable method of dealing with it
- the character, antecedents and community ties of the defendant
- previous bail record
- the strength of the evidence; and
- any other factors which appear relevant.

Paragraph 8 of the schedule provides for the court, where it has granted bail, to impose conditions where it appears to be necessary for the purpose of preventing the occurrence of any of the events mentioned in paragraph 2.

Most academic writers emphasise that decisions whether to remand accused people in prison or to release them on bail are among the most difficult and profound that a magistrate has to take—but, it is worth noting that in the author's own research, undertaken among magistrates on the Lincoln bench, only slightly more than half agreed with this statement. Home Office Research and Planning Unit Paper 65 pinpoints the difficulty as magistrates 'having to balance the right of the community—not to be exposed to unnecessary crime—and the right of the defendant—not to lose his liberty without due cause'. This balancing act involves forecasting someone's future behaviour on the basis of often limited information and under pressure of time (Doherty and East, 1985, showed that in their sample 62 per cent of bail applications took less than two minutes and 96 per cent less than ten minutes). Partly as a result, it seems, approximately two out of five people remanded in custody are finally given a prison sentence. There is some non-custodial disposal in two out of five cases, and one out of five is found not guilty. There is no cause for complacency here: those found not guilty receive no compensation for the disruption to their lives because somebody made the 'wrong guess'. It can be added that the figure for those not given a custodial sentence should be treated with care: some may have served sufficient time on remand to cancel out the appropriate prison sentence and there is some evidence that sentencers sometimes take the view that 'enough is enough' and dispose of the matter through a non-custodial sentence, whereas imprisonment would have been the outcome if the person had not been remanded in custody to start with.

How do courts considering bail or custody come to their decision? Block (1990), himself a magistrate, describes the process thus:

- are there substantial grounds for believing that one or more reasons exist why bail should be denied? If the answer is 'no' then unconditional bail must be granted. If the answer is 'yes' then the next question must be
- are there conditions of bail that would allay these grounds. If the answer is 'yes' then bail with appropriate conditions must be granted?

Raine and Wilson (1995) state that the proper process involves first deciding between bail or custody and only then, if bail is chosen, whether any conditions should be attached. Not the same process at all!

The position is complicated by practices which Raine and Wilson found. One stipendiary magistrate commented that, '. . . conditions are only frighteners to show you mean business', while several magistrates referred to conditions as being important in conveying messages to other parties. Occasionally, a condition to report regularly to a police station was imposed to remind the defendant about the discipline that the court expected and because it had the additional advantage of adding some 'structure' to the person's life. The imposition of conditions under each of these circumstances is unlawful.

They also found widespread recognition that 'bail with conditions' had come to be regarded as a 'middle ground' between unconditional bail and custody, perhaps as a concession to the Crown Prosecution Service who had opposed bail or because the bench did not want to appear soft. Needless to say this was not the legislature's intention.

Why should as many defendants as possible be released on bail? Firstly, come the serious financial and personal results which may flow from a period of custody. Jobs may be lost, rent not paid and eviction may follow with dire results for whole families. Secondly, preparation of a case for trial is much more difficult in custody. Contact with the solicitor is likely to be sporadic and, in fact, many lawyers cannot afford the time and send a clerk. There is evidence that a remand in custody can reduce the prospects of a non-custodial sentence. Two pieces of research by Brown (1990) and Hedderman (1991) illustrate this. Imogen Brown of the West Yorkshire Probation Service found that even when the gravity of cases were similar there was a much greater likelihood of a defendant who was remanded in custody receiving a custodial sentence than one who had been on bail. Carol Hedderman (of the Home Office) found that being remanded in custody was an important predictor of a later custodial sentence even when remand cases were matched with bail cases for such factors as nature, seriousness, previous convictions, employment status etc. There is also evidence to suggest that defendants who are remanded on bail are more likely to be acquitted than those in custody and this may be connected to the greater ease with which a case can be prepared.

The third point concerns the conditions in which remand prisoners are kept. In this connection it needs to be remembered that figures suggest that the average period on remand is over seven weeks and *Hansard* (13 April 1994) showed 190 prisoners on remand for over 18 months. There seems to be a belief that remand prisoners spend their time in conditions rather akin to a not very good hotel. Lord Windlesham, a former Chairman of the Parole Board paints a different picture:

The detainee gets up at the same time as the convict, he goes to bed at the same time, he takes exercise (one hour in 24) in the same place, he eats at the same time, is subject to the same discipline and the same loss of privacy, endures the same humiliating sanitation, the noise, the overcrowding . . . he is often held in a local prison where overcrowding is most acute . . . above all, the detainee is subject to uncertainty.

The privileges accorded to remand prisoners cannot outweigh these conditions. Lord Windlesham was writing in 1988, but in 1992 the then Director of the Prison Service was writing '. . . the regime for unconvicted prisoners . . . is often far worse than for the convicted'.

Conditions of bail
In theory, a court may impose any conditions that it sees fit, provided always that they prevent the defendant failing to surrender, committing an offence while on bail, interfering with witnesses etc. Generally courts are not very imaginative—although the author knows of one court that imposed a condition that a defendant must not dismount from his motor cycle while proceeding through a particular town on his way between home and work! Most of the time though courts tread a well worn path. A condition of residence at a specified address with the purpose of ensuring attendance at court is the most common: most research reflects a figure of around 70 per cent of conditional bail cases.

Of course it is difficult to refute the argument of Block (1990) that if a defendant intends to come to court he or she will do so wherever he or she is living: if they do not they will not let the small matter of an address stop them from absconding. Reporting to a police station appears in most research in about 17 per cent of cases (but for some reason in Lincoln in 30 per cent of cases). Again the intention is to ensure attendance at court but in these days of rapid travel a person could report and be anywhere in the world before his next reporting time, even if the police followed up his non-reporting.

Curfews are imposed in around 20 per cent of cases and are built on the proposition that if the defendant committed his last offence during the hours of darkness he or she could not possibly change his or her hours of operation. The 'door-step curfew' where bailees are obliged to present themselves on the doorstep if requested seems a more effective form of curfew. No contact with a named person or persons comes second to residence in popularity (46 per cent) and keeping away from a certain place in some 23 per cent of cases. With regard to the former, a solicitor informed the author that he is sometimes asked by defendants 'What if the person contacts me?' There seems to be no answer to this! Hucklesby (1994) makes the point that such conditions as 'Keep out of the city centre except to visit your solicitor by appointment or to attend court' are vague (where is the city centre?) and the chances of being seen are fairly slight. If, however the defendant is, say, seven feet tall or readily distinguishable in some other way, the condition may appear to discriminate against that particular defendant.

The breach of a bail condition is not an offence, and the police have been known to complain that when they do bring a defendant back to court for breach the person is usually bailed again with the same or a similar condition. A significant number of magistrates would like to see it become an offence, but as Hucklesby writes, '. . . if the court has already decided that the case itself does not warrant a remand in custody it is difficult to argue that a breach of a condition, whatever the severity or motive, without further alleged offending behaviour, should result in a remand in custody'.

Raine and Wilson (1995) make an interesting point when they observe that in their research there were occasions when the conditions of bail were announced by the chairman in court but no grounds given, or they were only added after prompting by the clerk. This notion is institutionalised in the design of bail forms and 'speaking parts' where conditions either come before the grounds for them or to the left hand side of the page. This invites the conclusion that conditions are decided first and the grounds come after, as a rationalisation.

Police bail

A custody officer can grant bail and since the Criminal Justice and Public Order Act 1994, attach conditions to bail (with the exception of the requirement to reside at a bail hostel). The Runciman Commission on Criminal Justice (1993) made the very practical suggestion that the police's inability to give conditional bail meant that people were being brought before the court unnecessarily. However, there are difficulties. Magistrates attach conditions to bail on a judicial basis. There have been suggestions that the police may attach conditions more to serve their own interests. For example, there is little doubt that reporting conditions are not popular in police circles and this may colour the use of such a condition. In a private letter to the author a solicitor wrote:

> . . . since the police were given the power to impose conditional bail, their use of it seems to me to be inappropriate in far more instances than is the case with magistrates. That is not surprising when one considers that a single custody sergeant can make a decision about bail conditions whereas (usually) three magistrates make such a decision, with legal input from the clerk if necessary.

The police decision to detain in custody or grant bail is an important one because of its influence on the courts' decision. Jones (1985) found that in

89 per cent of cases where magistrates granted bail the defendant had been bailed by the police and in 90 per cent where the defendant had been remanded in custody he had previously been detained in police custody.

Offending while on bail

The subject of 'bail bandits', as they have been called, is an emotive one and needs to be looked at coolly. *Hansard* reports the late Michael Shersby MP as follows:

> The granting of bail to young men who constantly re-offend is known by the police as the revolving door syndrome. An individual is arrested, charged with an offence and then granted police bail. By the time that offence comes before the court, a period of some six months might have elapsed, during which the young person concerned will have probably committed numerous further offences, including burglary, which is now a major scourge of this country.
>
> 21 April 1993

The Northumbria Police carried out research in 1991 which showed that 23 per cent of all arrests were of people who were on bail for other offences, and that bailed defendants committed 40 per cent of detected crime in the area. The Avon and Somerset police produced a figure of around 30 per cent of crimes committed being by people already on bail. In 1992, Patricia Morgan carried out a study of all the work being done on this subject for the Home Office. She concluded that the methodology used by both the Northumbrian and the Avon and Somerset forces resulted in a serious overestimate (Put briefly the former was based on arrests not on charges, the latter had used charges but neither had taken into account 'not guilty' outcomes). The actual conviction rates for offenders on bail was between ten and 12 per cent, which was very much the same result as the figures produced by similar research in 1978. The Home Office did find that offending on bail is more prevalent among male offenders, aged 17 to 20 years with previous convictions who are on bail for vehicle related crime and burglary.

Only about a third of all crime is detected and we have no idea how much of the undetected two-thirds is committed on bail, so that we have to accept that we can actually draw no very firm conclusions about the extent of bail banditry. It appears that the best we can do is to say that about 90 per cent of those granted bail are not convicted of an offence while on bail. Section 66 Criminal Justice Act 1993, makes it mandatory for the fact that an offence hes been committed on bail to be treated as an aggravating factor 'no matter how trivial, unconnected or irrelevant to the instant offence' (Cavadino and Gibson 1993).

Bail or Custody?—Key Points

- The decision to remand in custody or on bail is governed by the Bail Act 1976.
- There is a presumption that a person will be granted bail.
- There are specified reasons for not granting bail and the grounds are linked to specific grounds.
- The court has to balance exposing the community to crime and the loss of liberty of the individual.
- This balance requires forecasting future behaviour on limited information and where there is often a lack of time.
- About 11,000 people are remanded in custody; less than 5,000 will receive a custodial sentence and over 2,000 will be found not guilty.
- Remanding in custody may result in financiai loss, greater prospects of a custodial sentence and an uncertain period of poor living conditions.
- Police as well as courts may grant bail or detain in custody: this has an important influence on final disposal.
- Research on offences committed on bail is inconclusive. Ninety per cent of those granted bail *do not* reoffend during the bail period.

• • •

PUNISHMENT AND SENTENCING

Yet one fact has been clearly established: the severity of punishments in no way diminishes the number of crimes.

Peter Kropotkin (1898)

In this section I will look at the justifications for *punishing* wrong-doers and then take an overview of sentencing without going into those details which are covered very adequately in other volumes. Probably most sentencers faced with the question 'What justifies the punishment that you are about to mete out?' would simply reply in terms of the relevant legislation which gives the power to impose penalties, but what we need to look at is the moral position that justifies the sentences that Parliament attaches to particular pieces of legislation—and the general requirement to impose a 'commensurate' (sometimes called 'proportionate') sentence. Perhaps the first question is whether we need to justify punishment at all. Surely the answer must be 'yes', since punishment is almost always the deliberate inflicting of suffering—or pain—and some moral justification is needed for doing that to another human being.

The two justifications usually cited are 'retribution' and what Walker calls 'reductivism'. The first is backward looking and based on the idea that the punishment is deserved; the second forward looking and based on reducing the incidence of crime in the future.

Reductionism

If it does indeed reduce crime, then the punishment will be justified by that form of moral reasoning known as utilitarianism (see *Chapter 2*). Given that utilitarianism depends on 'the greatest good for the greatest number' the reduction of crime will be to that end. There are, however, at least a couple of problems with that idea. It depends on a consensus of what is 'good' and, in a pluralist society, that will not be easy to decide. In addition, this approach seems to exclude reduced punishment on the basis of mitigating circumstances. If a sentence is lowered then it may not be the one that produces the greatest good.

There are a number of ways in which punishment may reduce crime. Proponents of 'punishment works' (or its variant 'prison works') usually stake their claim under one or more of the bases briefly considered under the next five sub-headings: *Deterrence; Reform (or Rehabilitation); Incapacitation; Retribution* and *Denunciation*.

Deterrence
The idea of deterrence is that an individual or the public at large is deterred, in some way or another, from criminal behaviour. There are thus two types of deterrence, *individual* and *general*.

With individual deterrence, someone who commits a crime is punished and the theory is that he or she finds this so unpleasant that they do not offend again. General deterrence involves people being stopped from committing crime by an awareness of what will happen to them if they do. Those who support the idea do so in the belief that a potential wrong-doer will calculate the risk involved and refrain for fear of punishment. Others dispute this and contend that the risk of punishment is irrelevant. Trivizas and Smith (1997) have demonstrated a short-term but sharp fall in the level of thefts of luggage from railway stations following terrorist incidents in stations. They conclude that there are two reasons for this: high police vigilance; and the danger of stealing luggage containing a bomb. This supports the first view of general deterrence. Walker (1980) distinguishes the two neatly: general deterrence relies on imagination while individual deterrence relies on memory.

But does punishment deter? Individual deterrence is difficult to measure and as already pointed out, only some three per cent of crimes end in successful prosecutions so it is difficult to draw any useful conclusion. Davies *et al* (1995) have shown that over half of offenders are reconvicted within two years of sentence and the rate varies only slightly for different types of offence. There is some evidence that punishment may actually increase the risk of offending. This is through 'labelling' (*Chapter 6*), and, in so far as imprisonment is concerned, we have all heard the expression 'university of crime'. In 1982, West actually suggested that if a boy offends, the best way to prevent him re-offending is not to catch him in the first place!

Cavadino and Dignan (1992) agree that a system of punishment has a general deterrent effect. They cite as an example the deportation by the Germans of the entire Danish police force during the Second World War. The incidence of theft and robbery rose spectacularly. Nevertheless, general deterrence is difficult to establish. The tendency is to emphasise the severity of punishment as a deterrent—sometimes nearly as crude as 'double the punishment, halve the crime'. But there is evidence that it is the certainty and immediacy of punishment that deters. Felton (1994) refers to touching a hot stove. The pain, though minor, is certain and quick, but the experience assuredly deters. But if you are burned once every 500 times you touch the stove and the pain is not felt until five months later the deterrent effect will be much less. Beccaria was making much the same point when he wrote 'Certainty of punishment . . . will always make a stronger impression than the fear of another which is more terrible but combined with the hope of impunity'.

Another difficulty noted by Beyleveld (1990) is that the vast majority of people have no conception of the likely penalty for particular offences. Perhaps problems of deterrence are well illustrated by the Kirkholt Burglary Project, where 70 per cent of burglars asserted: 'You don't think about whether you will get caught and what will happen to you then', although, inconsistently, 51 per cent said that 'If you know that you will get a tough sentence then you will think twice'.

Reform (or Rehabilitation)

The hope here is that punishment will improve the wrongdoer's character and reduce the likelihood of further criminal behaviour. The hey day of rehabilitation was in the late 1960s with its emphasis on individual sentences tailored to the needs of the offender rather than in proportion to the seriousness of the offence; indeterminate sentences with 'cure' as the factor determining release, and treatment programmes. By the 1970s this was seen as unjust (those who played the 'cure game' were released earlier than prisoners who wouldn't, even if the crime was worse), and ineffective because the lesson that prison was unlikely to reform offenders was slow to be learned and, perhaps above all, expensive. Martinson (1974) caught the mood when writing 'Nothing, or almost nothing works'. Today, this view is seen as over pessimistic and there is a realisation that some forms of treatment do work for some offenders. This can be seen in the new forms of probation orders with, for example, the Probation Service confronting offenders with their wrongdoing.

Incapacitation
Here the offender is prevented, or at least discouraged, from offending either temporarily or permanently. Incapacitation covers a wide range of punishments from the practice, in some countries, of chopping off the hands of thieves to disqualification from driving. Most people probably think of imprisonment as the major form of incapacitation and as Feeley and Simon (1992) write:

> If the prison can do nothing else, incapacitation theory holds it can detain offenders for a time and this delays their resumption of criminal activities – if sustained for enough time and for enough offenders significant aggregate effects in crime can take place *although individual destinies are only marginally altered.* (Emphasis supplied)

Retribution
This justification for punishment is simply that the wrongdoer 'deserves it'. It is morally right to return evil for evil. It has been written of the retribution theory that

> It may at least be said that if it is an assertion of the right to inflict all the pain which a criminal act may merit, it is the denial of the right to inflict on any human being any unnecessary pain.

This is at the root of 'just deserts' to which we will return, just as retribution is at the root of the whole of the 'law and order ideology' and the 'get tough on criminals' policy which seems to have been embraced from the mid-1990s by both the political right and left.

Where can we find a moral base for retribution? Although, to many people, it seems 'right' and accords with commonsense it is not easy. Some writers have based a justification on the idea of a 'social contract' (see, generally, *Chapter 2*). All citizens are bound together by a nexus of rights and duties which include obedience to the law of the land. Criminal behaviour disturbs the equilibrium and an unfair advantage over others is gained—and it is punishment which restores the balance. This resonates with Beccaria's writings (*Chapter 2*). Others have criticised this theory by pointing out that it is only valid if, to employ a modern and over-used expression, you start with 'a level playing field'. If you do not, then restoring equilibrium can have no meaning—but we know that most offenders start from a position of social disadvantage and punishment then increases inequalities.

Murphy (1979) has gone so far as to say that 'modern societies lack the moral right to punish'. We need not agree, but the most devout follower of retributionism must be concerned at the lack of consistent sentencing practice that bedevils our system and, of which, more later.

Denunciation

This is well summarised by Lord Denning when giving evidence to the Royal Commission on Capital Punishment:

> The punishment for grave crimes should adequately reflect the revulsion felt by the great majority of citizens for them. The ultimate justification for punishment is not that it is a deterrent, but it is the emphatic denunciation by the community of a crime.

Cavadino and Dignan (1992) refer to two versions of the denunciation theory. The first they term 'instrumental denunciation', which is a form of reductivism in that it may reduce crime by reinforcing the 'conscience collective' of society, to use Durkheim's phrase, and ensure that members refrain from criminal behaviour. The second is 'expressive denunciation' which is simply an expression of society's abhorrence of crime.

Pointing out that no system is entirely retributivist or reductivist the authors refer to the 'promiscuously eclectic mixture' in the English system. This is epitomised in *R v Sargeant* (1974) where, in the Court of Appeal, the justifications were described as retribution, deterrence, denunciation and reform—while the White Paper, *Crime, Justice and Protecting the Public* which gave birth to the Criminal Justice Act 1991 pronounced 'denunciation and retribution' as the first objectives for all sentences. But the 1991 Act itself refers to sentences 'commensurate with the seriousness of the offence', i.e. it appears to be based on retribution.

Sentencing Generally

Cavadino and Dignan wrote, in 1992, 'The single most distinctive feature of the English sentencing system is the breadth of discretion that is conferred on sentencers at all levels within the system'.

Because of this breadth of discretion, the factors which might influence sentencing become of importance. Remembering that 95 per cent of criminal cases are dealt with to finality in the magistrates' courts where offenders are sentenced by lay, unpaid volunteers, that is where I will look. Despite efforts to broaden the base of the magistracy it seems as if the criticism that JPs are, 'overwhelmingly middle-aged and middle-class' still holds good and is likely to remain so for good reasons, for example the time that is required to be made available. In 1955 Nagel wrote that the average criminal case 'represented a conflict of social groups in that the defendant generally tended to be a member of the lower-middle or working class, and the prosecutor a member of the upper-middle or upper class enforcing laws promulgated by upper-middle and upper class legislators'. One hopes that in the last 20 or so years there have been some changes, but the main point, that there is usually a huge gulf between sentencer and offender remains. What is of perhaps greater concern is the studies that have shown that the principal determinant of sentencing practice within a bench is the 'sentencing culture', some of which may well 'trickle down' from the justices' clerk. New magistrates are socialised into this culture. Cavadino and Dignan believe that the ideology that gives rise to this culture is the belief in the uniqueness of both the magisterial role and of each individual case. Sentencing then becomes a 'craft or mystery whose rites are known only to initiates' and consequently almost immune from criticism.

Rutherford (1994) quotes Walter Miller:

> Ideology and its consequences exert a powerful influence on the policies and procedures of those who conduct the enterprise of criminal justice . . . Ideology is the permanent hidden agenda of criminal justice.

Are factors such as this an explanation for the inconsistencies of sentences to which we have referred? In 1994, in research into magistrates' courts, Moxon and Hedderman found a wide range of differences in sentences:

- conditional discharges ranged from nine to 31 per cent of cases
- fines ranged from 31 to 67 per cent; and
- immediate custody ranged from three to nine per cent.

In 1992 Liberty researched the number of adults sent to custody from various magistrates' courts between 1981 and 1990 and found a range between 17 per cent at South Tameside (Greater Manchester) to 0 per cent at Eastleigh (Hampshire). It is difficult to believe that these differences are due entirely to differences in types of cases.

The 'just deserts' approach to sentencing, enshrined in modern legislation, has a formidable pedigree. It was Aristotle who wrote 'Like cases should be treated alike and unlike cases should be treated proportionate to their differences'. Essentially this means that the seriousness of the offender's crime ought to be the decisive factor in sentencing. Andrew Asworth (1994) suggests that the rise of 'just deserts' is explained by:

- the loss of faith in rehabilitation;
- awareness of the limits of deterrence; and
- increasing concern about fairness and the 'rights' of people sentenced.

He also points to the importance of 'proportionality', which includes two distinct concepts, often overlooked. The first is 'ordinal proportionality' which involves ideas on how one crime should be punished compared not only with similar criminal acts but others of a more or less serious nature. How do we rank robbery, rape, the supply of drugs and so on? The second is 'cardinal proportionality' which refers to the maximum level and the actual sentencing range for a particular offence. These depend on cultural and social conditions. As an example of cardinal proportionality it would not be thought right today to send someone to prison for five years for a trivial theft though once the punishment would have been even greater.

The 'just deserts' approach clearly has the advantage of seeming fair because to the public at large it gives the offender what he or she deserves, and it should promote certainty and consistency through the various guidelines, but it is not without its problems. One of these is how to deal with previous convictions and the question 'Does "just deserts" demand sentencing for just the present offence or is seriousness influenced by previous offences?'. The legislature has had difficulty with this. The notorious section 29(1) Criminal Justice Act 1991 (as originally enacted) provided that 'an offence shall not be regarded as more serious . . . by reason of any previous convictions' but, after much public criticism, and not least from the Magistrates' Association, section 66 Criminal Justice Act 1993 allowed the court to take account of previous convictions when assessing the seriousness of the present offence. The essential problem of balancing consistency and flexibility in sentencing practice remains.

Over the last 40 years and particularly since the 1970s non-custodial sentences as 'alternatives to custody' have been pressed on sentencers. Voss (1990) describes these alternatives as 'penalties which following conviction and sentence and allow the offender to spend part or all of his or her sentence in the community and outside prison establishments. The thrust of this move was to reduce the prison population—something it failed to do. Because these 'alternatives to custody' were seen by sentencers—and by the public—as 'soft options', the government increased their punitive aspect and called them 'punishments in the community'. Whether this has made them more credible is a matter for debate. The headline 'Criminal Walks Free' when, in fact, a community service order has been imposed, suggests that the media, at least, equate punishment with *prison*. Courts now have a bewildering array of community penalties from which to choose, based on a central core of probation, community service and combination orders.

Some of the theoretical views on the move away from prison are worth noting. Scull (1977) argued that the trend—and he included the community care movement—was little to do with humanitarianism but all to do with the worsening fiscal crisis which brought with it the need to decrease public expenditure on problem populations. The weakness of his argument is that, in fact, the law and order budget has actually increased.

Cavadino and Dignan are surely correct when they suggest that penal policy is a complex product of political, ideological and economic pressures. Cohen (1985) sees the movement not as a transformation away from the 'carceral' but as an extension whereby control based on discipline is dispersed into the rest of society. Mathieson takes this 'dispersal of discipline' theory further and sees a focus on control of whole groups and categories of people, not just on individuals. As an example of what he means, he writes:

> TV cameras on subway stations and in supermarkets, the development of advanced computer techniques in intelligence and surveillance . . . all this is something we have begun to get, and have begun to get used to.

Punishment and Sentencing—Key Points

- Justifications for punishment are *reductionism* and *retribution*.
- Reductionism looks forward. It is based on the idea that crime can be reduced through:
  - — deterrence
  - — reform or rehabilitation
  - — incapacitation.
- Retribution looks backwards and is based on the notion that punishment is deserved: this is at the root of 'just deserts'.
- The English sentencing system has been described as a 'promiscuously eclectic mixture'.
- Sentencers have a breadth of discretion and concerns are expressed about disparity between sentences.
- Alternatives to custody have been pressed on sentencers particularly in the 1980s and up until 1992 (when all penalties became sentences/punishments in their own right). They were frequently attacked as 'soft options' although now described as 'punishment in the community'.
- Some commentators see the movement away from custody as a dispersion of discipline in society.

PRISONS

> If the Prison Service contains [the] prisoner in conditions which are inhumane or degrading . . . then a punishment of imprisonment which was justly imposed will result in injustice . . . it is the Prison Service's duty to look after prisoners with humanity. If it fulfils this duty, the Prison Service is partly achieving what the court must be taken to have intended when it passed a sentence of imprisonment.
>
> Woolf Report (1991)

A well-known sound bite is former Tory home secretary Michael Howard's assertion that 'prison works'—closely followed by Labour prime minister Tony Blair's assurance that his government would be 'Tough on crime, tough on the causes of crime'.

As a society we seem to show an increasing support for imprisonment as a punishment. In 1945 there were about 15,000 people in prison in England and Wales: by 1970 that figure had grown to 39,000 and in 1999 this stands at around 65,000 (which is about 10,000 above the true capacity of the system). It is proposed that an extra £43 million will be spent within the next two years to cope with demand (and an extra £250 million has been made available to improve regimes). The Crime (Sentences) Act 1997, which provides that, but for 'exceptional circumstances', offenders convicted of a second 'serious offence' will receive a mandatory life sentence and those convicted of a third class A drug trafficking offence will be sentenced to seven years in prison—and the new so-called 'three strikes' provision in relation to burglary which means a mandatory three years—is expected to increase the prison population by at least 4,000 over the next few years. A projection published in January 1999 forecast that the total prison population in 2006 would be 68,900. The early indications are that these projections may turn out to be optimistic.

In 1995, 20,200 people were given custodial sentences by magistrates and in 1996 the figure was 22,200. Most magistrates will say how rarely they send anyone to prison, but there are about 30,000 of them and the fact is that one in three receptions into custody is from a magistrates' court. The figures for the Crown Court were 39,800 and 42,700 respectively.

In 1992 the number of prisoners sharing a cell was 7,251; by the middle of 1997 it was 10,296; and by 1999 it is expected to be 16,000. In addition, whatever explanation can be put forward, the fact is that the United Kingdom imprisons more people per head of population than any other West European country. The average cost of keeping someone in custody for a year is around £37,000.

Historically, the prison—as we know it—is a comparatively recent social experiment which only began 200 years ago (although different forms of prisons in the sense of private dungeons or keeps existed earlier). Prior to that, a sentence of imprisonment was rare and the people imprisoned were either debtors or prisoners awaiting trial. The main forms of punishment were execution (in the century after 1688, 200 new capital offences were made, giving rise to the so-called 'Bloody Code') or transportation. In 1755 the American War of Independence seriously hampered transportation as a form of punishment and was a stimulus to the changeover to prisons. It is interesting to note that such was the shortage of prison space that two floating prisons or 'hulks' were moored in the Thames and became home to 2,000 convicts. Around the end of the eighteenth century and the beginning of the nineteenth came the 'great transformation' as physical suffering was replaced by imprisonment as the dominant form of punishment ('From the corporal to the carceral', as Foucault described it). The Prisons Act 1877 took the control of prisons away from local justices and put it into the hands of central government (until 1 April 1993 when the Prison Service attained 'next steps' agency status).

At the time of the 1877 Act, there were about 30,000 people in prison; by the beginning of the First World War there were 9,000—and the figure fluctuated between 10,000 and 12,000 up to the outbreak of World War II.

What are prisons for? Firstly, there is their social function, then their function within the criminal justice process, and then the goals of prisons as institutions. Only in the light of all these purposes can it be decided— at least provisionally—if, indeed, prison works.

The social function
The Norwegian penologist, Thomas Mathiesen (1974) (who at the outset it should be said, is convinced that prison should be abolished) has suggested that the emergence of prisons as the dominant form of punishment was to do with the social functions that they performed in advanced capitalist societies. These he described as the:

- *expurgatory function*: those who are unproductive and disruptive are contained where they can do the least damage
- *power-draining function*: those who are contained in prisons are not only prevented from interfering with the normal processes of production but are unable to exercise any responsibility as prisoners
- *symbolic function*: those on the outside are able to distance themselves from people who are publicly labelled as prisoners
- *action function*: people are reassured that something is being done about the problem of law and order; and

- *diverting function*: because the ultimate sanction of imprisonment tends to be reserved for the lower working class, concern by members of society tends to be focused on the band of offences which they commit and this diverts attention from the serious social harm caused, for example by companies compromising on safety standards in the pursuit of profit and other corporate crimes.

Function within the criminal justice system

Morgan (1994) describes the prison function as:

- *custodial:* as well as people serving sentences (see *punitive function* below), this refers also to those prisoners held on remand and those convicted but not yet sentenced, probably because they are awaiting pre-sentence reports
- *coercive:* this is almost entirely in connection with fine defaulters who will be released on meeting their obligation, or when their period of custody in lieu of payment is served
- *punitive:* this is the great majority who are serving a sentence ordered by the court.

The function of the institution

From the point of view of prison institutions themselves there may be a difficulty. Changes of policy about the function of imprisonment have led to what has been called an ideological crisis. In 1964, Prison Rule No 1 stated

> The purpose of the training and treatment of convicted prisoners shall be to encourage and assist them to lead a good and useful life.

I have noted earlier the waning of confidence in the treatment model during the 1970s (see *Punishment and Sentencing*). It was argued that while the treatment and training paradigm was perceived by sentencers as a real and desirable outcome of imprisonment then they would continue to use this form of punishment although the outcome was actually a delusion. A committee under Mr Justice May (1979), with a wide remit to enquire into the Prison Service, agreed that the 'rhetoric of treatment and training has had its day and should be replaced'. But what would fill the vacuum?

Two criminologists, Roy King and Rod Morgan (1980), argued for a system based on 'humane containment'. By this they meant:

- minimum use of custody
- minimum use of security necessary to safeguard the public; and

- normalisation; by which they meant that the same standards should govern the life of offenders in prison as if they were in the community.

The May Committee rejected humane containment as a 'means without an end' and replaced it with the notion of 'positive custody'. This involved:

- keeping prisoners in custody in a way that is both secure and positive
- creating an environment which would assist them to respond to society in a way that was as positive as possible
- preserving and promoting self-respect
- minimising the harmful effects of removal from normal life; and
- preparing them for and assisting them on discharge.

King and Morgan contended that positive custody had 'no real meaning' and one writer described the two viewpoints as 'warehousing and zookeeping' respectively. Neither were taken up.

By 1983 this high rhetoric had been replaced by a statement of tasks whereby the director general of the Prison Service had to use, with maximum efficiency, the resources of staff, money, building and plant and the service was to provide '. . . as full a life as possible consistent with the facts of custody and help prisoners keep in touch with the community'.

Baroness Stern, formerly director of the National Association for the Care and Resettlement of Offenders (and later the International Centre for Prison Studies and Prisoners Abroad) described this as 'A sad decline from the high ideals of changing human beings to giving prisoners a regular bath and ensuring that they get their visits from their families'.

In 1988, a 'mission statement' was produced which reflects perhaps, the same retreat from high idealism:

Her Majesty's Prison Service serves the public by keeping in custody those committed by the courts. Our duty is to look after them with humanity and help them lead law abiding and useful lives in custody and after release.

Critics were not slow in pointing out the number of prisoners who escaped from custody, the dreadful conditions in which many prisoners were kept, the lack of facilities for work and education and the number of assaults by prisoners on other prisoners and on staff. All this seemed a long way from the above mission statement. By 1990, the Home Office was referring to the danger of prison being an 'expensive way of making bad people worse'.

Rutherford (1993) described the new prison ideology as 'expedient managerialism' which he defined as a situation which gives 'priority to narrowly-defined performance measures and to short-term trouble shooting over any articulation of purposes and values'. There is a great temptation to enquire of the reader whether this strikes a chord as relevant to any other parts of the criminal justice system.

On 1 April 1990, all those problems which Cavadino and Dignan (1992) had called the penal crisis—the rapidly rising prison population; the overcrowding; the conditions; the staffing; the security; the control; and the lack of justice inside the prisons—came to a head in Strangeways, Manchester, where a prison riot, largely among remand prisoners, left one person dead, many injured and £30 million worth of damage. Disturbances followed in 30 other penal institutions and many of these involved remand prisoners.

The government acted swiftly and the Woolf Report was published in February 1991. It consisted of two parts; the first was written by Lord Justice Woolf (as he then was) himself and described the events, the second looked at the problems and proposed remedies. In that part, Lord Woolf was assisted by His Honour Sir Stephen Tumim, former HM Chief Inspector of Prisons. The report emphasised the need for security (preventing prisoners from escaping), control (preventing disturbances) and justice (reasonable conditions, and due process in the treatment of prisoners and in decision-making about them). These, the report considered, should be at the right level and the right balance should be sought. Some of the main recommendations of the report were:

- closer co-operation between the various parts of the criminal justice system
- a director general should be appointed who would be the operational head and in day-to-day charge of the service
- increased delegation of responsibility for governors
- an enhanced role for prison officers
- a 'contract' for each prisoner setting out rights and responsibilities
- there should be no more prisoners in a particular prison than is provided for by the certificate of normal level of accommodation
- sanitation for all inmates
- better links with families through the use of community prisons By this expression the report visualised prisons next to the main centres of population, with the facilities and accommodation capable of holding most prisoners throughout their sentence. The walls of such prisons would be more permeable to facilitate the maintenance of ties with the community. This sounds not dissimilar to King and Morgan's 'normalisation'

• different treatment for remand prisoners with lower security.

In 1992, Shaw wrote that:

> The genius of the Woolf Report lies in its ability to locate a grave breakdown in law and order and in the context of the longstanding problems of the prison system, overcrowding, decrepitude, poor management and a lack of justice and humanity.

After Woolf

The Criminal Justice Consultative Council and its local committees were set up soon after Woolf. The government also acted speedily in the whole area of prison visits and contact with the community, providing telephones and ending the routine censorship of mail. A director general was appointed, Derek Lewis, but he was sacked in October 1995 in a disagreement with the home secretary over accountability and the difference between policy and day-to-day operations (subsequent directors being Sir Richard Tilt and Martin Narey). Woolf's recommendations about limiting the number of people held in individual prisons to the certified normal accommodation level was rejected because of the huge input of resources that would be required— in 1994, for example Leicester Prison was 77 per cent over its capacity. The government acted speedily to deal with the problem of 'slopping out' which had been the cause of much resentment. However, this was done in most cases by taking the middle cell of three, and dividing it into two—providing toilet facilities for the cell on either side. Some prisoners resented 'sleeping in a lavatory' and, of course, the loss of the cells (each of which, in effect, became two toilets) added to the problem of overcrowding.

It is difficult not to agree with the assessment of Cavadino and Dignan above that the future verdict on the report will be in terms of a missed opportunity rather than a turning point in the history of prisons.

The abolitionists

I cannot leave the topic of prisons without reference to the abolitionists. Mathieson, whom I mentioned earlier, wrote 'The prison system as a way of thinking . . . emphasises violence and degradation as a method of solving inter-human conflict'. Abolitionists go further than simply criticising the existence of prisons. Willem De Haan (1990) bases his view on the moral conviction that social life should not and cannot be regulated by criminal law. Other ways of dealing with problematic situations, behaviours and events should be developed. Punishment is not the appropriate reaction to crime. We also need to break the crime control equals punishment equals imprisonment nexus. The prison system, De Haan believes, is counter-productive, difficult to control and itself a major social problem. 'Prisons are places where a lot more harm is done than is necessary or legitimate.' So what are the alternatives, even if one agrees with much of what De Haan says? He starts from the argument that there is no such thing as 'crime'. In fact, he writes,

> . . . the very form of criminal law, with its conception of "crime" (not just the contents of what is at a given time and place defined into that category, but the category itself) and the ideas of what is to be done about it, are historical "inventions".

De Haan acknowledges that there are all sorts of unfortunate events, more or less serious troubles and conflicts which result in suffering, harm or damage. These must be taken seriously but not as 'crimes'. He goes on, 'When we understand crime as a socially constructed phenomenon any simplified reaction to crime in the form of punishment becomes problematic'. Abolitionists believe that it is ridiculous to claim that one pain can or, indeed, ought to be compensated for by a state-inflicted one. De Haan sees 'redress' as an alternative to punishment and crime. Claiming redress invites an open discussion of what the appropriate response ought to be.

> Without fixation on individual guilt, responsibility and punishment, "crimes" would appear as "conflicts", "accidents" or "problematic events" to be dealt with in a more reasonable and caring way by using forms of conflict management which are not exclusively geared towards individuals and confined to the limitations of criminal law in the books as well as in action. (Steinert, 1986)

To the charge that all this is naive and idealistic, De Haan replies that the abolitionists approach is more realistic in that social problems and conflicts are seen as inherent to social life and that it is an illusion that the criminal justice system can protect us against these events. We might as well deal with them pragmatically rather than through the concepts of 'crime', 'guilt' and 'punishment'.

He does acknowledge that the problems of 'the really bad and the really mad remain'. As a last resort he believes that depriving someone of their liberty might be unavoidable.

Prisons—Key Points

- The number of people in prison continues upward: four times as many since 1945 and one and a half times since 1970.

- The United Kingdom imprisons more people per head of population than any other European country.
- To the question 'What are prisons for?' there are three answers from different perspectives: social function, place in the criminal justice system and goals of the institution.
- Mathieson suggests that the social function is connected with the role that prisons play in advanced capitalist societies: that those who are in prison, who are mainly from the lower working class, are contained where they do the least damage and those outside can distance themselves and be reassured. All this diverts attention from the causes of serious social harm.
- Morgan describes the function as: custodial, coercive and punitive.
- In 1964 the function of imprisonment concentrated on training and treatment.
- In 1979 the May Committee considered that this was rhetoric that had had its day and replaced it with 'positive custody' but this was not taken up.
- King and Morgan argued for 'humane containment': minimum use of custody and security and 'normalisation'.
- What actually happened Rutherford describes as 'expedient managerialism' which has little, if any, purpose or values.
- Serious disturbances in 1990 led to the Woolf Report which emphasised the need for security, control, and justice.
- Some of its recommendations were implemented and some not: Cavadino and Dignan call it a missed opportunity.
- Abolitionists like De Haan criticise the very existence of prisons and do not believe that social life should be controlled by the criminal law and that we should break the crime control-punishment-prison circle through redress.

• • •

CRIME PREVENTION AND COMMUNITY SAFETY

"Community solutions" are all grounded in massive assumptions about human society and social relations, while designing out crime presupposes rational risk — averse offenders.

Francis Heidensohn (1989)

As Pease (1994) points out, 'It would in principle be possible to prevent all crimes at a stroke, simply by repealing the relevant statutes'. This means, he continues, '. . . that when we are considering crime prevention the only link between the events that we want to prevent is that they are proscribed by statute. What will prevent one type of crime, let us say an opportunist burglar, will not prevent false accounting'. There are three broad approaches to crime prevention:

- *Primary prevention:* This is the variety that comes most readily to mind. It is concerned with the protection of the target and is effective before or while the offence is committed either, in the former case, by stopping the crime or, in the latter, by slowing offenders down and increasing the chances of their being caught. It has no reference to criminals themselves, or to potential criminals. It works only at the site of crime.

- *Secondary prevention:* This is concerned not so much with the prevention of crime as the prevention of criminality and its focus is on changing people.

- *Tertiary prevention:* This is prevention as practised by the criminal justice process. Someone serving a prison sentence is prevented from committing a crime during the period of his or her incarceration; someone disqualified from driving is prevented from offences in connection with motor vehicles.

Primary prevention

This section concentrates on primary prevention and 'community solutions'. In an article, 'Situational Crime Prevention: Theory and Practice' (1980) Ron Clarke attacks the 'dispositional bias' of much criminological theory. By this he means, in particular, those positivist theories outlined in *Chapter 3*—although he also includes 'labelling' (*Chapter 6*)—which show that people are born with, or acquire, a 'disposition' to behave in a consistently criminal manner. These theories are unhelpful as far as crime prevention is concerned and pay little attention to the fact that crimes may be of a bewildering variety, from the relatively trivial to the most serious and that there are only a relatively small number of criminally disposed individuals. In addition, says Clarke, the bulk of crime is committed by people who would not ordinarily be thought of as criminal. The search for a single cause of crime is as fruitless as that for a single cause of disease.

Attention really began to be paid to primary crime prevention in 1976 with the publication by the Home Office of *Crime as Opportunity*. The stimulus was strange. Research showed that when natural gas was substituted for toxic gas in the home not only did the number of suicides using gas fall but so did the total number of suicides by all methods. Potential suicides, who one would have thought had a strong 'dispositional bias', apparently did not seek alternatives. If the reduction in opportunity to commit suicide reduced the numbers, would not the same apply to crimes?

Clarke conceived of crime as the outcome of choices and decisions based on the perception of costs and benefits—and exhibiting a degree of rationality: hence the name 'rational choice theory'. (Readers will recollect 'routine activities theory' with its notion of motivated offender, suitable victim, and absence of capable guardian which is not dissimilar to this: see *Chapter 3*). Situational crime prevention concentrates on reducing or removing the benefits by reducing the opportunities and making the rewards more difficult to obtain.

Among the most obvious measures that the situationists would support are *target hardening* (as it is known) or the removal of the target altogether. Some of the first work in this field was on the prevention of car thefts by the introduction of steering locks. In the United Kingdom, this was initially on new cars only, so that the number of thefts of old cars increased; an interesting example of 'displacement'. Thefts from telephone kiosks were greatly reduced by the use of steel coin boxes. A more recent example has been the use of electronic surveillance (EAS) or electronic tagging of articles of merchandise.

As far as *target removal* is concerned examples include those music shops which only display the box but keep the CD or tape at a central point, the use of cardphones to eliminate money being stored in telephone boxes, and prepayment tokens for gas and electricity meters.

The attractiveness of articles can also be reduced. Property marking has a variety of purposes: it makes the detection of offences easier; it assists in returning articles to the rightful owner; and it makes resale of an article more difficult (in the Kirkholt research, mentioned at p.37, nearly half of the burglars disposed of the items which they had stolen through shops or other dealers).

In 1985, Laycock persuaded 72 per cent of the residents of three neighbouring villages in South Wales to take advantage of free marking equipment, window stickers and extensive media publicity. There was a 40 per cent reduction in thefts but a later follow-up suggested that this might well have been due to the press attention rather than to the marking.

The public often express the view that the best crime prevention measure of all is *more policemen on the beat*. Unfortunately, there is little evidence that this is true. As Clarke and Hough point out, the average police officer is very unlikely to come across a crime which is actually in progress and Lea and Young contend that heavy police patrols can in fact increase crime by alienating citizens with the police coming to be perceived as 'the enemy'.

Architecture and crime prevention

It is worth making a brief reference to the fascinating subject of architecture and crime. Oscar Newman referred to the need for 'defensible space' in housing schemes. He referred to four features:

- *territoriality*: the area should be divided into 'zones of influence' creating a private image which discourages outsiders. This can be done by coloured surfaces or humps only allowing room for one car
- *surveillance*: easy observation of the area should be possible with overlooked entrance lobbies and no blind areas where people can hide
- *image*: this refers to the necessity of avoiding the look of low cost uncared for houses; and
- *environment*: the area should give the impression of being in a wider crime free area, i.e. it is surrounded by a 'moat'.

Neighbourhood Watch

Neighbourhood Watch schemes have become popular as a means of crime prevention. In 1994 there were said to be over 130,000 schemes with around five million members. Some critics doubt the accuracy of these figures on the grounds that as there is no definition of a Neighbourhood Watch scheme (which is thus meaningless) and, in any case, many schemes only exist on paper. They also point to the lack of evidence that such schemes actually prevent crime—and suggest that they only work in those middle-class areas where crime rates are low; and that schemes simply displace crime and police resources (the latter from areas where they are more badly needed). All this is very negative. The effect of any crime prevention scheme is difficult to measure because it involves something that *did not happen,* and there can be little doubt that in watch areas the fear of crime *has* been dramatically reduced. It must be accepted that in areas of public sector housing, growth of these schemes has been slow. An interesting point is raised by Shapland and Vagg (1987) who examined what they called 'informal watching' (watching, noticing, direct action) and noted how localised this informal social control was. A street was 'too large a unit'. This suggests that Neighbourhood Watch schemes may be misdirected.

Some criticisms

The chief criticisms of the primary approach to crime prevention is that the benefits to society are minimal. What is needed is to change people, because there is 'little point [in] situational crime prevention [if it] shuffles crime from one area to the next but never reduces it'. (Heal and

Laycock, 1986). Frankly, what is required, say the critics, is social engineering.

Crime displacement
The idea of crime displacement was first examined by Reppetto (1976) and developed by others so that we now have the following classification:

- *spatial:* if the opportunity does not exist in one place (where perhaps there are CCTV cameras in operation) opportunities are taken elsewhere
- *temporal:* if the time is inappropriate (because, for example the attendant is in the car park) the criminal tries at another time
- *tactical:* a different method is tried
- *crime type:* another type of crime is tried; and
- *different perpetrator:* one person makes his or her rational choice in one direction and does not attempt the crime, but another person may come to a different conclusion.

If crime displacement was total, then criminology could, like economics, be rightly called 'the gloomy science'. Fortunately, not all crime is displaced and consequently some crime, at least, is prevented. Wheeler refers to the fact that all our lives are lived with an economy of effort and if an activity becomes so difficult to complete with a reasonable amount of effort, we give up. Crime is no different. Ekblom refers to the 'ratchet effect' of crime prevention: as more and more targets are made secure so that the ratio of risk to reward increases. Barr and Pease (1992) though, warn against the real risk of city centre TV driving crime onto working class estates which become 'crime fuses', and plead for an equality of resource allocation.

Secondary crime prevention
Supporters of social crime prevention aim to prevent people drifting into crime by improving social conditions, strengthening community institutions and enhancing recreational, educational and employment opportunities. John Bright in *Crime Prevention: The British Experience* (1991) points out that the situationalists are quite unable to prevent, for example many violent crimes, domestic violence, child abuse and racially motivated crime. He shows that crime is not evenly spread but found particularly in inner, urban, run down areas and council estates. In high crime areas informal social controls which inhibit criminal behaviour are lacking and a subculture (*Chapter 6*) where personal status is enhanced by criminal activity may exist. It is from this analysis that the policy of improved housing and recreational facilities, schools where

pupils are motivated and offered a sense of achievement and improved chances of employment flow. The problem is that all these policies are costly and the results take a long time to be seen. Their saving grace is that they are of intrinsic worth whether or not they reduce crime.

The work of Elliot Currie (1991) can be taken as a paradigm of this viewpoint. He believes that 'market society' where the pursuit of private gain increasingly becomes the organizing principle for all social life is a fertile ground for the growth of crime because:

- it increases inequalities and concentrates economic deprivation
- it weakens the machinery of informal support, mutual provision and socialisation and supervision of the young. 'If you're having tough times you can't lean on your neighbours because they're having tough times too'
- it causes stress and fragmentation of families: Currie refers to an American situation (which may be relevant in the UK), where families can only stay afloat by long hours of work and even more than one job, so that parents have little leisure time, are living under stress and absent from home most of the time; and
- it creates a culture of competition and urges a level of consumption that it cannot fulfil for all.

Currie's solution is a labour market policy that provides all citizens with, not only the competence and skill to work, but the opportunities. He also advocates the reduction of extreme inequalities, an active, supporting child and family policy, strategies to reduce conflict between families and adequate child care systems for working families. He concludes:

> What all this means is that real social crime prevention, like the prevention of other social ills is now more than ever dependent on our capacity to build more effective movements for social action and social change.

From the British left realist perspective, Jock Young sees the answer in the reduction of relative deprivation through meaningful work for a fair wage, decent housing and leisure facilities. He also advocates an emphasis in the police role in fighting crime, not acting as traffic cops, lost property agents or the secret social services.

In contrast to this view, we can look at the writings of Charles Murray and his concept of the 'underclass'. Murray contrasts the underclass with the poor, who only lack money. On the other hand, the underclass are defined by their behaviour, their homes which are littered and unkempt, their inability to keep a job for more than a few weeks and their ill-schooled and ill-behaved children. He describes three ways to identify an underclass: 'illegitimacy, violent crime and drop-out from the labour force'. His gloomy conclusion about dealing with this problem is that:

> Providing educational opportunities or job opportunities doesn't do it. Training programmes don't reach the people who need them. We don't know how to make up for the lack of good parents . . . Most of all, we don't know how to make up for the lack of a community that rewards responsibility and stigmatises irresponsibility. It's not money we lack but the capability to social-engineer our way out of this situation.

Tertiary crime prevention
As indicated elsewhere (see p.80), due to attrition, the criminal justice process—whilst it has a significant part to play—cannot hope to prevent crime in any comprehensive way. Only around two or three per cent of crime actually results in a conviction, and the majority of offenders who are convicted reoffend within two years.

Crime prevention—a note
Throughout this section, I have used the term 'crime prevention' but the Home Office Standing Conference on Crime Prevention prefers 'community safety' because it is open to a wider interpretation which encourages greater participation from all sections of the community in the fight against crime and this is reflected in the provisions of the Crime and Disorder Act 1998. It is worth noting that Crawford (1998) warns that

> In the search for practical solutions to immediate problems [in crime prevention and community safety] we have tended to become blind to the more enduring political, cultural, ethical and social issues.

Crime Prevention—Key Points

- Primary prevention works by increasing costs or reducing benefits and works only at the site of crimes.
- Critics argue that it only reduces some crime and benefits to society are minimal.
- Not all crime that is prevented is displaced in some way.
- Secondary prevention involves improved social conditions through, for example housing, schooling, employment.
- Critics like Murray do not believe that social engineering works.
- Tertiary crime prevention involves restrictions imposed by the criminal justice process, but has little significant effect.

• • •

WHITE COLLAR CRIME

The public tend to be more afraid of being mugged, raped or robbed by a stranger in the street than they are of being killed on a commuter train, poisoned at a wedding party or seduced by a host of misleading advertisements, cheap bargain offers or bogus investment claims.

Hazel Croall (1992)

Most of us—and certainly those addicted to police dramas on TV such as *The Bill*—have a conception of offending built on street crime, with a background of working class people on housing estates and only very rarely of plush offices and wealthy businessmen. Nevertheless, Stephen Box (1983) has argued that white collar crime is *more* prevalent and has a *greater cost* to society than conventional crimes. Wilson (1975) expresses a different point of view when he writes:

People do not bar and nail shut their windows, avoid going out at night or harbour deep suspicions of strangers because of unsafe working conditions or massive consumer fraud.

It is a matter for each of us to decide how we compare offences for seriousness; burglary of a dwelling house at night with, say, breaches of safety regulations by the Union Carbide Company that led to 2,600 deaths in Bhopal; the Zeebrugge disaster and the sinking of the *Marchioness* with the loss of 193 and 51 lives respectively; the fact that three out of five deaths at work are due to violations of the Health and Safety at Work Act 1974; or the misery caused by the BCCI banking collapse. It is not easy to grade such incidents as against other serious crimes, or each other.

The field of 'white collar crime' was pioneered in the 1940s by Edwin Sutherland whose differential association theory has already been mentioned: see *Chapter 6*. His interest was largely due to the fact that he wanted to show that that theory could account for *all* forms of criminal behaviour, i.e. that it was a *general* theory of crime. He defined white collar crime as 'crimes committed by persons of high social status and respectability in the course of their occupation'. This definition has been roundly criticised. The social status of offenders should not be part of a definition; thefts can be carried out at all levels of the business hierarchy and unsuspecting customers can just as well be 'ripped off' by the local corner shop as by the supermarket. In any case, how does one determine respectability? A second major criticism was that Sutherland failed to distinguish between crimes committed *for* an organization and those *against* it.

Even now, not all textbooks are consistent with their terminology. The problem boils down to finding something in common between, say, fiddling a few pounds at work and releasing onto the market a drug known to be unsafe, or insider trading.

White collar crime can be sub-divided into 'occupational crime' and 'organizational crime' (sometimes called 'corporate crime': the former term is generally considered to be more exact because it can include both private and public organizations).

Occupational crime consists of those 'offences committed by individuals in the course of their occupations against their employers'. The figures are staggering. Karen Gill (1994) reports, for example that the British Retail Consortium estimate theft by staff in the retail industry exceeds £550 million in value per year. As further examples, she cites airline staff fiddling drinks on flights to the tune of £2 million and a hotel, restaurant and public house chain where staff fiddles represent three per cent of annual turnover.

Organizational crime could be defined as 'illegal corporate behaviour in order to advance organizational goals'. Another term, 'crimes of the powerful' is often used by writers trying to make a political point and is probably best confined to state crimes such as gross violations of Human Rights.

It is obvious that occupational crimes come nearer to our usual idea of crime than do organizational crimes, but some characteristics are common to both (Croall: 1992)—though more so in some cases than others:

- *low visibility*: these crimes take place under cover of the routine work of the organization by people who have a right to be at the scene; victims are often unaware that an offence has been committed
- *complexity*: sometimes the crime might be a simple case of theft but it may also be extremely complex with the person involved making use of his or her existing expertise in finance, technology, or law. The crime might also involve many employees in a web of deceit.
- *diffusion of responsibility*: it may be difficult to decide who is responsible and this is particularly true of organizational offences. There may be several layers of management involved. Those higher up can claim that their orders were ignored and those lower down that they were following orders. The offence may not contain any element of intent but just neglect in failing to follow regulations.
- *diffusion of victimisation*: Box (1983) cites the contrast between an old lady having five pounds snatched from her purse and 25

million customers paying one penny more for orange juice diluted beyond the level permitted by law. The customer is likely to shrug off the penny, lose sight of the illegal profit and worry more about the old lady.

- *detection and prosecution*: white collar crime is often difficult to detect and, even when it *is* detected, it is difficult to prove. Seemingly, only a tiny proportion of offenders are prosecuted.
- *lenient sanctions*: the absence of violence means and the fact that offenders are not perceived as dangerous means that few offenders are sent to prison, and fines are often 'derisory'. Levi goes so far as to suggest that judges are reluctant to pass heavy sentences on 'their own'.
- *ambiguous laws*: the complexity of much white collar crime is such that 'it is often difficult to capture the essence of offences in legislisation' (Croall, 1992). Tax evasion, for example is incredibly complicated and the law has to keep up with avoidance schemes and as one loophole is closed another is found.
- *ambiguous criminal status*: many of the 'offences' are not seen as *really* criminal. Sometimes they are offences of strict liability (i.e. where no proof of intent is required). Two major textbooks published in 1990 nicely illustrate the dichotomy. Clarke, a British author, takes the view that white collar crimes often '. . . result from duress, incompetence, negligence, lack of training . . . sheer muddle-headedness . . . not to be handled in the same way as ordinary crime'. From across the Atlantic, the author of the Foreword to a different volume writes that white collar crime '. . . is without doubt more dangerous, both in physical and fiscal terms, than street crime'.

White collar crime is of particular interest to the criminologist because of the question whether the theories of conventional crime should be applicable to white collar crime or whether they demand a different approach. If they do there cannot be a general theory of crime. Presumably, those responsible for the BCCI fraud (the collapse of the Bank of Credit and Commerce International as a result of misjudged/unauthorised investments and a lack of supervision/control) were not suffering from maternal deprivation, zinc deficiency or some problem with their chromosomes! Before coming to that topic it might be as well to look briefly at law enforcement and white collar crime.

Law enforcement and white collar crime
Law enforcement is generally in the hands of bodies like the Health and Safety Executive, Environmental Health officers and Trading Standards officers. There are two opposing viewpoints about enforcement which

can be described as the *compliance* model and the *policing* model. Those who support the former will say that the acts that are being dealt with are different from 'crimes' and are best dealt with through advice. Companies are not 'amoral calculators' and do not deliberately commit offences but are 'political citizens' with an interest in the best for society generally. The regulatory agencies should be consultants rather than policemen; with prosecution used as a last resort. In any case, this is the best way to prevent future incidents and it is much cheaper than the lengthy investigations that prosecution would demand: the unsuccessful prosecution in the case of the Zeebrugge ferry disaster is said to have cost £10 million. The other view is that white collar crime *is* crime and ought to be dealt with in the same way as other crimes—and failure to do this weakens the law.

Pearce and Tombs (1990) argue that corporations *are* amoral calculators and any view that they can do anything else other than attempt to maximise long-term profitability is untenable. Within a capitalist system that makes them criminogenic because it forces them into exerting as much control as possible over their operating environment and pushes them into violating regulations. It is easy to overstate these differences because, as already discussed, the police have a discretion in relation to prosecution in other areas and the views expressed above are extreme ends of a continuum.

Understanding white collar crime
The early theories of crime concentrated very much on lower class crime and looked for the reasons in individual biological, psychological and personality traits etc. With the advent of radical criminology (*Chapter 7*) came the 'break': the introduction of the assertion that previous theories demonstrated a class bias and that the lower classes were criminalised at the expense of the middle and upper classes because their crimes were largely ignored. Sutherland applied his theory of 'differential association' to white collar crime. Many businessmen learn to commit crimes to enhance the company when they would not consider any other sort of criminality. They learn the 'realities of business' and receive an excess of definitions favourable to the violation of the law over definitions that are unfavourable.

Helpful categories used by Hazell Croall (1992) are as follows:

Rotten apples
Just as the positivists attempted to find out what made some people criminal and others not, so there is a tendency to find individuals at fault in an organization so as to draw attention away from the organization itself. What makes these 'rotten apples'? Gross (1978) finds in the very qualities likely to make successful businessmen the same qualities that

are likely to make them criminal. He says that top executives are 'ambitious, shrewd, and possessed of a non-demanding moral code'. Box (1983) believes that when such people get near the top of a large company they are 'in a high state of preparedness to commit corporate crime should they perceive it as being necessary for the good of the company'.

Clinard (1983) attempts to distinguish businessmen who will break the law from those who would not. He thought that those more likely to engage in unethical practices came from those interested in financial prestige and quick profits; the entrepreneurial who maximised profits and the mobile executives recruited from outside the company. These contrasted with the professional managers, the 'fiduciary' managers committed to a service ethic and managers promoted from the ranks. Although Box (1983) dismisses these as 'Dallas type sketches' there is support for example in the work of Quinney (1963) who found that pharmacists with a professional orientation committed virtually no offences compared with the more business orientated pharmacists. Croall sums up the focus on individuals as providing 'only a very partial view of criminality' which can '. . . divert attention from wider organizational or structural problems'.

Criminal organizations
Some organizations possess illegitimate opportunity structures which simply means that if employees have access to money or goods then, subject to the way the business is organized and the degree of supervision, theft becomes possible. Mars (1982) classifies occupations on the basis of the chances they provide for fiddling:

- *hawk jobs:* these are jobs such as sales and professional ones where workers have a high degree of autonomy, which produces many opportunities for fiddling
- *donkey jobs:* where workers have little freedom, are separated from colleagues and are closely supervised and have little opportunity for fiddling, for example supermarket cashiers
- *wolfpack jobs:* which rely on teamwork and provide opportunities for highly organized fiddles; and
- *vulture jobs:* like those in the hotel and catering industry where there is competition and uncertainty exploited by management and workers.

Workplace subcultures
Fiddling and pilfering may be tolerated where it has become part of the subculture (see, generally, *Chapter 6*). Management may even tolerate fiddling as an alternative to a pay increase and if they then take a

tougher line they may be rewarded by a militant stance among the work force. Mars (1982) cites an example of this among the baggage handlers at Heathrow who, following prosecutions of colleagues for theft, went on strike.

Enterprise and crime
Mars (1982) suggests that 'There is only a blurred line between entrepreneuriality and flair on the one hand and sharp practice and fraud on the other'. Croall (1988) quotes a car dealer convicted for turning back an odometer who said he was '. . . in the business of buying and selling cars'. No other explanation was felt necessary. Cressey (1986) refers to the excuse, 'honesty is the best policy but this is business'. These kinds of argument suggest that the law actually gets in the way of the proper pursuit of business goals—very similar to the 'techniques of neutralisation' noted by Matza (p.57).

Crime and the business environment
Box (1983) applies anomie theory (*Chapter 4*) to the position where, because of the business environment, legitimate means of profit-making are blocked. Then the organization's aims may be pursued by illegitimate means as the company seeks innovative ways to make profits in the new and threatening situation. This must follow when, writes Box, the main long-term goal is the maximisation of profit. Among the environmental problems may be: competitors' finding a break-through product; employees searching for better working conditions or high wage settlements; consumers turning to other products or the government producing new regulations. Box refers to 'the strain towards innovative behaviour which can stretch over the spectrum law-abiding-law-avoiding-law-evading-law-breaking'.

White collar crime and the future
Hills (1988) asks for '. . . greater public understanding of the relationship between corporate decision-making and human suffering'.

In most cases when corporations are fined the amount is derisory. It can be suggested that fines should be made realistic but not so as to threaten jobs in the organization. Some people have gone so far as to advocate a sort of means enquiry form for companies.

Custodial sentences are rare in these cases although, as in the Lyme Bay canoeing disaster where the company was charged with manslaughter and the managing director sentenced to three years imprisonment, it is sometimes the outcome.

Among other suggestions proposed by academic writers are: a period of probation for an offending company (as is available to some American courts) where a team of experts oversees the probation order and monitors standards; a community service order, in which the company makes reparation by, say, building a new school (Box) and an idea from Pearce and Toombs, a penalty points system, similar to that for drivers, complete with 'MOTs' and disqualification.

White Collar Crime—Key Points

- Sutherland's much criticised definition of white collar crime was in terms of 'high social status' and 'respectability' of those committing crimes in the course of occupation.
- A more usual definition is in terms of occupational crime which is by employees against employers and organizational crime (or corporate crime) which is for the organization.
- Stephen Box argues that white collar crime is more prevalent and has a greater cost than conventional crime.
- Enforcement of organizational crime is through the compliance model (which is advisory) or policing model (through prosecution).
- Qualities that make a good businessman may be similar to those of a criminal.
- For many reasons, much occupational crime remains undiscovered.
- Box uses concept of anomie to explain organizational crime in an adverse environment.
- Future possibilities include probation, community service orders and penalty points systems for companies.

Bibliography

Ackers, R L, (1973), 'Problems in the Sociology of Deviance', *Social Forces* 46

Adler, F, (1975), *Sisters in Crime*, New York: Macgraw Hill

Alderson, J, (1998), *Principled Policing*, Winchester: Waterside Press

Allport, F, (1924), *Social Psychology*, Boston: Houghton Mifflin

Ashworth, A, (1994) (originally 1983), 'Criminal Justice and Deserved Sentences' in *A Reader on Criminal Justice*, Lacey, N, (ed.), Oxford: Oxford University Press

Baldwin, J D, (1990), 'The Role of Sensory Stimulation in Criminal Behaviour' in *Crime in Biological, Social and Moral Contexts*, Ellis, L, and Hoffman, H, (eds.), New York: Praeger

Bandura, A, (1986), *Social Foundations of Thought and Action*, Englewood Cliffs NJ: Prentice Hall

Barr, R and Pease, K (1992), 'Crime Displacement to Crime Displacement' in *Crime Policy and Police*, Evans, D (ed.), London: Routledge

Becker, H, (1963), *Outsiders: Studies in the Sociology of Deviance*, New York: Free Press

Berkowitz, L, (1972), 'Frustrations, Comparison and other Sources of Emotional Arousal as Contributors to Social Unrest', *Journal of Social Issues*, 28

Beyleveld, D, (1980), *A Bibliography on General Deterrence Research*, London: Saxon House

Bittner, E, (1974), 'Florence Nightingale in Pursuit of Willie Sutton: A Theory of Police' in *The Potential for Reforming Criminal Justice*, Jacob, H (ed.), Beverley Hills: Sage

Bottomley, A, Coleman, C, (1981), *Understanding Crime Rates*, Farnborough: Saxon House

Bottomley, A, and Pearse, P, (1986), *Crime and Punishment: Interpreting the Data*, Milton Keynes: Open University Press

Bottoms, A, Mawby, R, and Zanthos, P, (1998), 'A Tale of Two Estates' in *Crime and the City*, Downes, D, (ed.), London: Macmillan

Bottoms, A, McLean, J, (1976), *Defendants in the Criminal Process*, London: Routledge

(1994), 'Environmental Criminology' in *The Oxford Handbook of Criminology*, Maguire, M, Morgan, R, and Reiner, R, (eds.), Oxford: Oxford University Press

Box, S, (1981), *Deviance, Reality and Society*, London: Holt, Rinehart and Wilson

(1983), *Power, Crime and Mystification*, London: Tavistock

(1987), *Recession, Crime and Punishment*, London: Macmillan

Braithwaite, J, *Crime, Shame and Reintegration*, Cambridge: Cambridge University Press

Braithwaite, J, and Pettit, P, (1990), *Not Just Deserts: A Republican Theory of Criminal Justice*, Oxford: Clarendon Press

Brantingham, P J, and Brantingham, P L, (eds.), (1989), *Patterns in Crime*, New York: Macmillan

Brown, D, Ellis, T, and Larcombe, K, (1992), *Changing the Code: Police Detention under the Revised PACE Codes of Practice*, Home Office Research Study No. 129: London: Home Office

Brownlee, I, (1998), *Community Punishments*, London: Longman

Burgess, E, (1916), 'Juvenile Delinquency in a Small City', *Journal of the American Institute of Criminal Law and Criminology* 6

Butler, A, (1982), *An Examination of the Influences of Training and Work Experience on the Attitudes and Perceptions of Police Officers*, Bramshill Police Staff College

Cavadino, M, and Dignan, J, (1992), *The Penal System*, London: Sage

Cavadino, P, and Gibson, B, (1993), *Bail: The Law, Best Practice and the Debate*, Winchester: Waterside Press

Christiansen, K, (1968), 'Thresholds of Tolerance in Various Population Groups Illustrated by Results from the Danish Criminologic Twin Study' in *The Mentally Abnormal Offender*, de Reuch A, and Porter R (eds.), Boston: Little Brown

(1974) 'Seriousness of Criminality and Concordance Among Danish Twins' in *Crime, Criminology and Public Policy*, Hood, R, (ed.), New York: Free Press

Clarke, M, (1990), *Business Crime: Its Nature and Control*, Cambridge: Polity Press

Clarke, R, and Hough, M, *Crime and Police Effectiveness*, London: Home Office

Cloward, R, Ohlin, L, (1960), *Delinquency and Opportunity: A Theory of Delinquent Gangs*, New York: Free Press

Clinard, M, (1983), *Corporate Ethics and Crime*, Beverley Hills: Sage

Cohen, A, (1955), *The Culture of the Gang*, New York: Free Press

(1966), *Deviance and Control*, Englewood Cliffs: Prentice Hall

Cohen, S, (1980), *Folk Devils and Moral Panics*, London: Martin Robertson

(1985), *Visions of Social Control*, Cambridge: Polity Press

Coleman, A, and Gorman, L, (1982), 'Conservatism, Dogmatism and Authoritarianism in British Police Officers' in *Sociology*, February

Cortes, J, B, and Gatti, F, M, (1972), *Delinquency and Crime: A Biopsychological Approach*, New York: Seminar Press

Crawford, A, (1998), *Crime Prevention and Community Safety*, London: Longman

Cressey, D, (1986), 'Why Managers Commit Fraud', *Australia and New Zealand Journal of Criminology*, 19

Croall, H, (1988), 'Mistakes, Accidents and Someone Else's Fault: The Trading Offender in Court' in *Journal of Law and Society*, 15

(1992), *White Collar Crime*, Buckingham: Open University Press

Currie, E, *International Developments in Crime and Social Policy*, London: NACRO

Davies, C, (1994), 'Does Religion Prevent Crime?: The Long Term Relationship Between Crime and Religion', *Informationes Theologiae Europae*

Davies, M, Croall, H, and Tyrer, J, (1995), *Criminal Justice*, London: Longmans

Dixon, D, Bottomley, A, Coleman, C, Gill, M, and Wall, D, (1989) 'Reality and Rules in the Construction and Regulation of Police Suspicion', 17 *International Journal of the Sociology of Law* 185

Doherty, M, and East, R, (1985) 'Bail Decisions in Magistrates' Courts' in *British Journal of Criminology* 25(3)

Douglas, M, (1992), *Risk and Blame: Essays in Cultural Theory*, London: Routledge

Downes, D, (1996), *The Delinquent Solution*, London: Routledge and Kegan Paul

Downes, D, Rock, P, (1988), *Understanding Deviance*, Oxford: Oxford University Press

Dunning, E, (1990), 'Sociological Reflections on Sport, Violence and Civilisation', *International Review for the Sociology of Sport* 25

Dunning, E, Murphy, P, Williams, J, and Maguire, J, (1984), 'Football Hooliganism in Britain Before the First World War' in *International Review Journal, Sociology of Sport,* 19

Dunning, E, Murphy, P, and Williams, J, (1986), 'Spectator Violence at Football Matches: Towards a Sociological Explanation', *British Journal of Sociology* 37

Eaton, M, (1987), 'The Question of Bail: Magistrates' Response to Applications for Bail on behalf of Men and Women Defendants' in *A Reader in Criminal Justice* Lacey, N, Oxford: Oxford University Press

Ekblom, P, (1987), *Preventing Robberies at Sub-Post Offices,* London: Home Office

Eysenck, H, (1987), 'Personality Theory and the Problem of Criminality' in *Applying Psychology to Imprisonment,* McGurk, B, Thornton, D, and Williamson, M, London: HMSO

Farrell, S, Bannister, J, Ditton, J, (1998), 'Questioning the Measurement of the "Fear of Crime"' in *The British Journal of Criminology* 37

Farringdon, D, (1994), 'Human Development and Criminal Careers' in *The Oxford Handbook of Criminology,* Maguire, M, Morgan, R, and Reiner, R, (eds.), Oxford: Oxford University Press

Farrington, D, Dowds, E, (1985), 'Disentangling Criminal Behaviour and Police Reaction' in *Reactions to Crime: The Public, the Police, Courts and Prisons,* Chichester: Wiley

Farrington, D, and Morris, A, (1983), 'Sex, Sentencing and Reconviction', *British Journal of Criminology* 23

Feeley, M, Simon, J, (1992), 'The New Penology: Notes on the Emerging Strategy of Correction and its Implications', *Criminology* 30

Felson, M, (1992), 'Routine Activities and Crime Prevention Studies' in *Crime and Crime Prevention: Annual Review* 1

Ferri, E, (1901; English edition 1908), *The Positive School of Criminology,* Chigago: Kerr

Field, S, Southgate, P, (1982), *Public Disorder: A Review of Research and a Study in One Inner-City Area,* London: HMSO

Forrester, D, Chatterton, M, Pease, K, (1988), *The Kirkholt Burglary Prevention Project,* CPU Paper No. 13, London: Home Office

Foucault, M, (1991), *Discipline and Punishment: The Birth of the Prison* (trans A Sheridan), London: Penguin

Garland, D, (1997), 'Of Crimes and Criminals' in *The Oxford Handbook of Criminology,* Maguire, M, Morgan, R, and Reiner, R, (eds.), 2nd edition, Oxford: Oxford University Press

Gaskell, G, Benewick, R, (1987), 'The Crowd in Context' in *The Crowd in Contempory Britain,* Gaskell, G, and Benewick, R, (eds.) London: Sage

Genn, H, (1988), 'Multiple Victimisation' in *Victims of Crime: A New Deal?,* Maguire, M, and Ponting, J, (eds.), Milton Keynes: Open University Press

Gibbons, D, (1994), *Talking About Crime and Criminals,* Englewood Cliffs, New York: Prentice Hall

Gibbs, J, (1996), 'Conceptions of Deviant Behaviour' in *Pacific Sociology Review* 9

Gill, K, (1994), 'Fiddling in Hotel Bars' in *Crime at Work,* Gill, M, (ed.), Leicester: Perpetuity Press

Glaser, D, (1956), 'Criminality Theories and Behavioural Images' in *American Journal of Sociology* 61

Glueck, S, and Glueck, E, (1950), *Unravelling Juvenile Delinquency*, Oxford: Oxford University Press

Goddfredson, M, and Hirschi, T, (1990), *A General Theory of Crime*, Stanford: Stanford University Press

Gould, S, J, (1996), *The Mismeasure of Man*, Harmondsworth: Penguin

Green, G, (1990), *Occupational Crime*, Chicago: Nelson Hall

Grosse, E, (1978), 'Organizations as Criminal Actors' in *Two Faces of Deviance: Crimes of the Powerless and the Powerful*, Braithwaite, J, and Wilson, P, (eds.), Brisbane: University of Queensland

Gurr, T, (1970), *Why Men Rebel*, Princetown NJ: Princetown University Press

Haan, W de, (1990), *The Politics of Redress: Crime, Punishment and Penal Abolition*, London: Unwin Hyman

Hall, S, (1980), *Drifting Into a Law and Order Society*, London: The Cobden Trust

Hall, S, Critcher, C, Jefferson, T, Clarke, J, and Roberts, B, (1978), *Policing the Crisis*, London: Macmillan

Hall Williams, J, E, (1982), *Criminology and Criminal Justice*, London: Butterworths

Healy, W, Bronner, A, (1936), *New Light on Delinquency and Its Treatment*, Newhaven: Yale University Press

Heidensohn, F, (1989), *Crime and Society*, London: Macmillan

Hills, S, (ed.), *Corporate Violence: Injury and Death for Profit*, Totowa NJ: Rowman and Littlefield

Hirschi, T, (1969), *Causes of Delinquency*, California: University of Califomia Press

Holt, R, (1989), *Sport and the British: A Modern History*, Oxford: Oxford University Press

Hucklesby, A, 'The Use and Abuse of Conditional Bail' in the *Howard Journal* 33

Hudson, B, (1995), 'Restoration, Reintegration and Human Rights', Paper to the Howard League, *Punishment in the Year 2000*, Edinburgh
(1996), *Understanding Justice*, Buckingham: Open University Press

Hytner, B, (1981), *Report of the Moss Side Enquiry to the Leader of the Greater Manchester Council*

Jefferson, A, (1990), *The Case Against Paramilitary Policing*, Milton Keynes: Open University Press

Jones, P, (1985), 'Remand Decisions in Magistrates' Courts' in *Managing Criminal Justice*, Moxon, D, (ed.), London: HMSO

Keith, M, (1993), *Race, Riots and Policing London*, UCL Press

King, M, and Brearley, N, (1996), *Public Order Policing*, Leicester: Perpetuity Press

King, M, (1981), *The Framework of Criminal Justice*, London: Croom Helm

King, M, and Morgan, R, (1980), *The Future of the Prison System*, Farnborough: Gower

Kropotkin, P, (1898), *Words of a Rebel*, New York

Lambert, J, (1970), *Crime, Police and Race Relations*, Oxford: Oxford University Press

Lange, J, (1929; English translation 1931), *Crime as Destiny*, London: Allen and Unwin

Laycock, G, (1985), *Property Marking: A Deterrent to Domestic Burglary*, London: Home Office

Lea, J, and Young, J, (1993), *What Is to be Done About Law and Order?*, London: Pluto

Lee, J A, (1981), *Some Stuctural Aspects of Police Deviance in Relations with Minority Groups in Organizational Police Deviance*, Shearing, C, (ed.), Toronto: Butterworths

Lemert, E, (1972), *Human Deviance, Social Problems and Social Control*, Englewood Cliffs NJ: Prentice Hall

McBarnet, D, (1981), *Conviction, Law, the State and the Construction of Justice*, London: Macmillan

McConville, M, Sanders, A, and Leng, R, (1993), *The Case for the Prosecution*, London: Routledge

McGurk B, and McDougall, C, (1981), 'A New Approach to Eysenk's Theory of Criminality' in *Personality and Individual Differences*, Vol 2

Magee, K, (1991), 'The Dual Role of the Royal Ulster Constabulary' in *Beyond Law and Order*, Reiner, R and Cross, M, (eds.)

Maguire, M, (1994), 'Crime Statistics, Patterns and Trends' in *The Oxford Handbook of Criminology*, Maguire, M, Morgan, M, and Reiner, R, (eds.) Oxford: Oxford University Press

Mars, G, (1982), *Cheats at Work*, London: George Allen and Unwin

Marsh, P, Rosser, E, Harre, R, (1978), *The Rules of Disorder*, London: Routledge and Kegan Paul

Marshall, G, (ed.) (1994), *The Concise Oxford Dictionary of Sociology*, Oxford: Oxford University Press

Martinson, R, (1974), 'What Works?: Questions and Answers about Prison Reform' in *The Public Interest* 35

Mathiesen, T, (1974), *The Politics of Abolition*, Oxford: Martin Robertson

Matza, D, and Sykes, G, (1957), 'Techniques of Neutralisation: A Theory of Delinquency' in *American Sociological Review*

Matthews, R, (1992), 'Replacing "Broken Windows": Crime, Incivilities and Urban Change' in *Issues in Realist Cnminology*, Matthews, R, and Young, J, (eds.), London: Sage

Mays, J, (1954), *Growing Up in the City*, Liverpool: Liverpool University Press

Mednick, S, Gabriell W, and Hutchings, B, 'Genetic Factors in the Etiology of Criminal Behaviour' in Muncie, J, McLaughlin, E, and Langan, M (eds.), *Criminological Perspectives*, London: Sage

Melnick, M, (1986), 'The Mythology of Football Hooliganism', *International Review for the Sociology of Sport* 21

Mendlesohn, B, (1956), 'Une Nouvelle Branche de la Science Bio-psycho-sociale: Victimologie', in *Revue Internationale de Criminologie et du Police Technique*

Mellor, R, (1989), 'Urban Sociology: a Trend Report' in *Sociology* 23

Merton, R, (1968), *Social Theory and Social Structure*, New York: Free Press

Miers, D, (1989) 'Positivist Victimology: A Critique' in *International Review of Victimology* 1

Morgan, A, (1939), *The Needs of Youth*, Oxford: Oxford University Press

Morgan, R, McKenzie, I, and Reiner, R, *Police Powers and Policy: A Study of Custody Officers*, London, ESRC

Morris, T, (1957), *The Criminal Area: A Study on Social Ecology*, London: Routledge and Kegan Paul

Morrison, W, (1995), *Theoretical Criminology*, London: Cavendish

Moston, S, and Stephenson, G, (1993), *The Questioning and Interviewing of Suspects Outside the Police Station*, London: HMSO

Moxon, D, Hedderman C, (1994), 'Mode of Trial Decisions and Sentencing Between Courts', *Howard Journal* 33

Muncie, J, (1996), in *Criminological Perspectives*, Muncie, J, McLaughlin E, and Langan, M, (eds.), London: Sage

Murphy, J, (1979), *Retribution, Justice and Therapy*, London: Reidal

Murray, C, (1996), 'The Underclass' in *Criminological Perspectives*, Muncie, J, McLaughlin, E, and Langan, M, (eds.), London: Sage

Newman, O, (1972) *Defensible Space: Crime Prevention Through Urban Design*, London: Architectural Press

Northam, G, (1988), *Shooting in the Dark: Riot Police in Britain*, London: Faber

Nye, F, (1958), *Family Relationships and Delinquent Behaviour*, New York: Wiley

Olwens, D, (1987), 'Testosterone and Adrenaline: Aggression and Anti-Social Behaviour in Normal Adolescent Males' in *The Causes of Crime: New Biological Approaches*, Mednick, S A, Moffit, T E, and Stack, S, (eds.), Cambridge: Cambridge University Press

Packer, H, (1968), *The Limits of Criminal Sanction*, Stanford: Stanford University Press

Parkin, F, (1992), *Durkheim*, Oxford: Oxford University Press

Pearce, F, Tombs, S, (1990), 'Ideology, Hegemony and Empiricism: Compliance Theories and Regulations', *British Journal of Criminolgy* 30

Pearse, P, (1986), *Crime and Punishment: Interpreting the Data*, Milton Keynes: Open University Press

Pearson, G, (1994), 'Youth, Crime and Society' in *The Oxford Handbook of Criminiology*, Maguire, M, Morgan, and R, Reiner, R, (eds.), Oxford: Oxford University Press

Pease, K, (1994) 'Crime Prevention' in *The Oxford Handbook of Criminology* Maguire, M, Morgan, R, and Reiner, R, (eds.) Oxford: Oxford University Press

Peckam, A, (1985), *A Woman in Custody*, London: Fontana

Pfohl, S, (1985), *Images of Devaince and Social Contol: A Sociological History*, New York: McGraw-Hill

Piliavin I, Briar, B, (1964), 'Police Encounters with Juveniles' in *American Joumal of Sociology* Volume 69

Plummer, K, (1979), 'Misunderstanding Labelling Perspectives' in *Deviant Interpretations*, Downes, D, and Rock, P, (eds.), London: Martin Robertson

Policy Studies Institute, (1983), *Police and People in London*, London: PSI

Pollak, O, (1950), *The Criminality of Women*, Philadelphia: University of Philadelphia Press

Quinnney, R, (1963), 'Occupational Structure and Criminal Behaviour: Prescription Violations by Retail Pharmacists', *Social Problems* 11 (1970), *The Social Reality of Crime*, Boston: Little Brown

Raine, J, Wilson, M, (1995), *Conditional Bail or Bail with Conditions*, Birmingham: Birmingham University

Reckless, W, *The Crime Problem*, New York: Appleton Century Crofts

Reicher, S, (1984), 'The St. Paul's Riot: An Exploration of the Limits of Crowd Action in Terms of a Social Identity Model', *European Journal of Social Psychology* 14

Reiner, R, (1992), *The Politics of the Police*, Hemel Hempstead: Harvester Wheatsheaf

(1992), *Chief Constables*, Oxford: Oxford University Press

(1994), 'Policing and Police' in *The Oxford Handbook of Criminology*, Maguire, M, Morgan, R, and Reiner, R, (eds.), Oxford: Oxford University Press

Reiss, A, (1951), 'Delinquency as the Failure of Personal and Social Controls', *American Sociological Review*, Vol 16

Rennie, Y, (1978), *The Search for Criminal Man*, Lexington, Massachusetts: Lexington Books

Repetto, T, (1976), 'Crime Prevention and the Displacement Phenomenon' in *Crime and Delinquency* 22

Rex, J, and Moore, R, (1967), *Race, Community and Conflict*, London: Sage

Robins, D, and Cohen, P, (1978), *Knuckle Sandwich*, Harmondsworth: Penguin

Rose, R M, Bernstein, I S, Gorden, T P, and Catlin, S F, (1974), 'Androgens and Aggression' in *Primate Aggression: Territoriality and Xenophobia*, New York: Academic Press

Roshier, B, (1989), *Controlling Crime: The Classical Perspective in Criminology*, Milton Keynes: Open University Press

Runciman, W, (1966), *Relative Deprivation and Social Justice*, London: Routledge and Kegan Paul

Rutherford, A, (1993), *Criminal Justice and the Pursuit of Decency*, Winchester: Waterside Press

(1994) 'Penal Policy and Prison Management ' in *Prison Service Journal*, Issue 90

Rutter, M, (1972), *Maternal Deprivation Re-Assessed*, Harmondsworth: Penguin

Samenow, S, (1984), *Inside the Criminal Mind*, New York: Times Books

Sanders, A, and Bridges, L, (1990), 'Access to Legal Advice and Police Malpractice', *Criminal Law Review* 494

Schalling, D, (1987), *Personality Correlates of Plasma Testosterone Levels in Young Delinquents: an Example of Person-Situation Interaction in the Causes of Crime: New Biological Approaches*, Mednick, S A, Moffit, T E, and Stack, S, (eds.), Cambridge: Cambridge University Press

Schoenthaller, S, (1982), 'The Effects of Blood Sugar on the Treatment and Control of Anti-Social Behaviour: a Double Blind Study of an Incarcerated Juvenile Population', *International Journal for Biosocial Research* Vol 3

Scraton, P, (1985), *The State of the Police*, London: Pluto

Scull, A, (1977), *Decarceration, Community Treatment and the Deviant*, Englewood Cliffs NJ: Prentice Hall

Shapland, J, (1998), 'Fiefs and Peasants: Accomplishing Change for Victims in the Criminal Justice System' in *Victims of Crime: A New Deal*, Maguire, M, and Ponting, J, (eds.), Milton Keynes: Open Universuty Press

Shapland, J, and Vagg, G, (1987), 'Using the Police', *British Journal of Criminology* 27

Shaw, C, (1966), *The Jack Roller*, Chicago: University of Chigago Press

Shaw, S, (1992), 'Prisons' in *Criminal Justice under Stress*, Stockdale, E, and Casale, S, (eds.), London: Blackstone Press

Sheldon, W, (1949), *Varieties of Delinquent Youth*, London: Harper

Skolnick, J, *Justice Without Trial*, New York: Wiley

Smart, C, (1976), *Women, Crime and Criminology*, London: Routledge and Kegan Paul

Smelser, N, (1962), *Theory of Collective Behaviour*, New York: Free Press

Smith, M, *Violence and Sport*, London: Butterworth

Smith, M, (1986), *Crime, Space and Society*, Cambridge: Cambridge University Press

Sparks, R, Genn, H, and Dodd, D, (1977), *Surveying Victims*, London: Wiley

Stanko, E A, (1983), 'Fear of Crime and the Myth of the Safe Home: A Feminist Critique of Criminolgy' in Yllo, K, and Bograd, M, (eds.), *Feminist Perspectives of Wife Abuse*, London: Sage

Steinert, H, (1986), 'Beyond Crime and Punishment' in *Contempory Crises*, 10

Sutherland, E, and Cressey D, *Criminology*, Philadelphia: Lippincott

Szasz, T, (1997), *Psychiatric Slavery*, New York: Free Press

Tame, C, (1993), 'Freedom, Responsibility and Justice: The Criminology of the New Right' in *The Politics of Crime Control*, Stenson, K, and Cowell, D, (eds.) London: Sage

Tannenbaum, F, (1938), *Crime and the Community*, New York: Columbia University Press

Taylor, I, (1989), 'Hillsborough, 15 April 1989: Some Personal Contemplations', *New Left Review* 177

Taylor, I, Walton, P, and Young, J, (1973), *The New Criminology*, London: Routledge

Taylor, Laurie, (1971), *Deviance and Society*, London: Michael Joseph

Trivizas, E, and Smith, P, 'The Deterrent Effect of Terrorist Incidents on the Rates of Luggage Theft in Railway and Underground Stations', *British Journal of Cnminology* 37/1

Tierney, J, (1996), *Criminology*, Hemel Hempstead: Prentice-Hall

Tiger L, and Fox, R, (1971), *The Imperial Animal*, New York: Holt Rinehart and Winston

Uglow, S, (1998), *Policing Liberal Society*, Oxford: Oxford University Press

Vass, A, (1990), *Alternatives to Prison*, London: Sage

Vold, G, and Bernard, T, (1986), *Theoretical Criminology*

Waddington, D, (1992), *Contempory Issues in Public Disorder*, London: Routledge

Waddington, P, (1986), 'Mugging as a Moral Panic', *British Journal of Sociology* 37 (1987), 'Towards Paramilitarism: Dilemmas in Policing Civil Disorder', *British Journal of Criminology*
(1991) *The Strong Arm of the Law*, Oxford: Clarendon

Walker, N, (1972), *Sentencing in a Rational Society*, Harmondsworth: Penguin

Walklate, S, (1995), *Gender and Crime*, Hemel Hempstead: Prentice Hall

Wasik, M, Gibbons, T, and Redmayne, M, (1999), *Criminal Justice,* London: Longman

West, D, (1969), *Present Conduct and Future Delinquency,* London: Heinemann

West, D, and Farrington, D, (1973), *Who Become Delinquents?,* London: Heinemann

Wikstrom, P, (1991), *Urban Crime, Criminals and Victims,* New York: Springer-Verlag

Wiles, P, (1991), 'Criminal Statistics and Sociological Explanations of Crime' in Carson, W, and Wiles, P, (eds.), *The Sociology of Crime and Delinquency in Britain,* London: Martin Robertson

Wilkins, L, (1964), *Social Deviance,* London: Tavistock

Williams, K, (1991), *Textbook on Criminology,* London: Blackstone Press

Wilson, H, (1980), 'Parental Supervision: A Neglected Aspect of Delinquency', *British Journal of Criminology* 20

Wilson, James Q, (1975; revised 1983), *Thinking About Crime,* New York: Basic Books

Willis, C, (1983), *The Use, Effectiveness and Impact of Police Stop and Search Powers,* HORPU Paper No. 15, London: Home Office

Woolf, H, and Tumin, S (1991), *Prison Disturbances April 1990,* London: HMSO

Young, J, (1994) 'Incessant Chatter: Recent Paradigms in Criminology' in *The Oxford Handbook of Criminology,* Maguire, M, Morgan, R, and Reiner, R, (eds.) Oxford: Oxford University Press

(1995) 'Crime and Deviance' in *Sociology,* Haralambos, M, and Holborn, M, (eds.), London: Collins

Zedner, L, (1994), 'Victims' in *The Oxford Handbook of Criminology,* Maguire, M, Morgan, R, and Reiner, R, (eds.), Oxford: Oxford University Press

Zimbardo, P, (1969), 'The Human Choice: Reason and Order Deindividuation, Impulse and Chaos' in *Nebraska Symposium of Motivation,* Lincoln: University of Nebraska Press

Index

Introductory Series

The Criminal Justice System
An Introduction
by Bryan Gibson and Paul Cavadino.

The Magistrates' Court
An Introduction
by Bryan Gibson. Consultant Mike Watkins.

Youth Justice and The Youth Court
An Introduction
by Mike Watkins and Diane Johnson

Police and Policing
An Introduction
by Peter Villiers

The New Ministry of Justice
An Introduction
by Bryan Gibson

The New Home Office
An Introduction
by Bryan Gibson

A History of Criminal Justice
In England and Wales
by John Hostettler

The Pocket A-Z of Criminal Justice
by Bryan Gibson

Build your set at all good bookshops, online and via **WatersidePress.co.uk**

WATERSIDE PRESS
Putting justice into words

Milton Keynes UK
Ingram Content Group UK Ltd.
UKHW041849101023
430330UK00004B/266

9 781872 870427